18.95

KT-449-740

3

PETERLEE
COLLEGE LIBRARY

AC26-15

EAST DURHAM COLLEGE LIBRARY

UNIX® for DOS Users

97000250

This book is

-8. F

31. APR

UNIX® for DOS Users

Martin R. Arick

A Wiley—QED Publication

John Wiley & Sons, Inc.

New York • Chichester • Brisbane • Toronto • Singapore

005.13

PETERLEE
COLLEGE LIBRARY

AC26-15

UNIX is a registered trademark of UNIX System Laboratories, Inc.

MS-DOS and Microsoft Windows are registered trademarks of Microsoft Corporation.

SCO is a registered trademark of the Santa Cruz Operation.

HP-UX is a registered trademark of Hewlett-Packard Corporation.

OS/2, AIX, and RS/6000 are registered trademarks of the IBM Corporation.

AT&T System V Release 4 is a registered trademark of the AT&T Corporation.

SunOS and Solaris are registered trademarks of SUN Microsystems, Inc.

Publisher: Katherine Schowalter
Editor: Robert Elliott
Assistant Managing Editor: Angela Murphy
Text Design & Composition: Publishers' Design and Production Services

Designations used by companies to distinguish their products are often claimed as trademarks. In all instances where John Wiley & Sons, Inc. is aware of a claim, the product names appear in initial capital or all capital letters. Readers, however, should contact the appropriate companies for more complete information regarding trademarks and registration.

This text is printed on acid-free paper.

Copyright © 1995 by John Wiley & Sons, Inc.

All rights reserved. Published simultaneously in Canada.

This publication is designed to provide accurate and authoritative information in regard to the subject matter covered. It is sold with the understanding that the publisher is not engaged in rendering legal, accounting, or other professional services. If legal advice or other expert assistance is required, the services of a competent professional person should be sought.

Reproduction or translation of any part of this work beyond that permitted by section 107 or 108 of the 1976 United States Copyright Act without the permission of the copyright owner is unlawful. Requests for permission or further information should be addressed to the Permissions Department, John Wiley & Sons, Inc.

Library of Congress Cataloging-in-Publication Data

Arick, Martin.
    UNIX for DOS users / Martin Arick.
      p.   cm.
    Includes index.
    ISBN 0-471-04988-3 (paper : acid-free paper)
    1. UNIX (Computer file) 2. Operating systems (Computers)
  I. Title
  QA76.76.063A753 1995
  005.4'3—dc20   95-14629

Printed in the United States of America

10 9 8 7 6 5 4 3 2 1

ID No: 97000250

Dewey No: 005.13

Date Acq:

About the Author

Martin Arick does customer support and training for Kronos, a Massachusetts company that provides electronic timekeeping systems. He has worked with a wide range of UNIX systems for more than ten years. He holds both an MS and a PhD from Washington University in St. Louis.

Contents

Preface

This book came about because a number of people that I work with were complaining that their knowledge of DOS seemed of little use in understanding UNIX. I set about to write a book that would build upon their knowledge of DOS and enable them to be effective users of UNIX with a minimum of pain. Thus, this book starts with an examination of the philosophies underlying UNIX as compared to DOS. Chapters follow that examine each of the general areas of interest on a UNIX system, always introducing the topic by looking at the DOS equivalent operation, if there is one. The version of DOS referred to in this book is the one that Microsoft wrote, more properly called MS-DOS. For purposes of brevity and ease of reference, it will be referred to as DOS throughout this book.

This book is divided into several parts. The first part is designed to start users on the path to being effective users of UNIX by comparing DOS commands to the matching UNIX commands. Thus, the DOS system knowledge that users already have is used to get a quick start at learning UNIX. The second part is oriented toward moving users beyond that beginner's stage to the more advanced (and more effective) stage of using a UNIX system by examining commands that use the power of a UNIX system and are not available on a DOS system. Chapters covering UNIX networking are also included. One appendix of this book details comparisons in tabular format between DOS commands and UNIX commands both by name of command and by function.

The first chapter of this book compares in general terms both the style and user environment on a DOS system with that of a UNIX system. This first chapter also includes a look at the history of UNIX. The next chapter examines functions that do not exist on a standalone DOS system but which must be executed in order to do anything on a UNIX system—that is, signing on to a UNIX system. The concepts of user name and password are examined along with a top-level look at the interaction of the operating system, a terminal, and the kernel. The following two chapters describe how the UNIX file structure operates very much like the DOS file structure and uses that DOS knowledge to name files and directories. The next chapter examines text file manipulation commands, comparing the DOS version with the UNIX version. The next chapters address more advanced UNIX system topics with first a chapter on using the **vi** editor, next a chapter on running applications, and finally chapters on two of the shell programs available on UNIX systems: the Korn shell and the C shell. Chapters discussing receiving and sending electronic messages and working with diskettes on a UNIX system are presented next. Finally, a trio of chapters examining how multiple UNIX systems cooperate follows with chapters on UNIX networking, using TCP/IP commands, and a brief look at UNIX interactions with the Internet.

Each chapter in this book contains exercises designed to be performed at the terminal. You should do them. They reinforce the lessons that are discussed in the chapter. Often the exercise includes some questions that are meant to be thought provoking. I hope they are. Answers to all exercises (and questions) are found in Appendix A.

Being able to determine quickly which UNIX command is most like the comparable DOS command is the intent of Appendix B, where tables present comparisons of DOS and UNIX commands in several different ways.

One note on the style of differentiating between what appears on a terminal and the command one needs to enter at the terminal to cause output to occur: The convention used in this book is that output to the terminal is shown in italics, text that needs to be inputted at the terminal is shown in boldface, references to commands are shown in boldface, and references to files are shown in italics. Thus, **Enter login** is a string that appears on a terminal, **cd newdir** is a command that is entered on the terminal, and */usr/good/.login* is the name of a file.

At times special keys on the keyboard are pressed to cause certain functions. For example, the **Escape** key (Esc) is pressed to cause the **vi** editor to leave insert mode. Several types of control characters are used in UNIX systems and will be specified as "^D", often spoken as "Control d". For entering such a control character from the keyboard, you would press the Ctrl and D keys at the same time.

UNIX® for DOS Users

Comparisons of DOS and UNIX

OVERVIEW

One way to understand a new system, one with which you have little familiarity, is to understand its differences and relationship to a system that you know in some depth. DOS systems are found in business settings nearly everywhere and even in many homes; thus, many people have significant exposure to DOS. Comparing a DOS system with a UNIX system can be one way to use knowledge of DOS systems to better understand a UNIX system.

Comparing a DOS system with a UNIX system can be done on several different levels. This chapter will compare the overall architectural aspects and styles of DOS and UNIX systems. The next part of the chapter will discuss some general differences between DOS commands and UNIX commands. Finally, the history and future of UNIX will be discussed.

DOS VERSUS NETWORKED DOS VERSUS UNIX

Standalone DOS

DOS systems are not all alike; they can be generally categorized into two types of systems: *standalone systems* and *networked systems*. The standalone DOS system can be illustrated as shown in Figure 1.1 and consists of one processor with memory, one key-

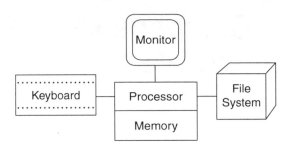

Figure 1.1.   Architectural view of standalone DOS system.

board, one monitor, and one file system. Most importantly, the system is operated by only one user at any time. Other users do not have access to the files in the file system. Programs started by the single user are the only programs executed on that processor. Physical media such as diskettes or tapes are used to make files available to other users.

Networked DOS

In business environments, the standalone DOS system is not the dominant system; instead, the networked DOS system has become the preferred system. As illustrated in Figure 1.2, the networked DOS computer system features a processor with memory and a local file system for each user and a server, accessed by users, that provides files shared among many users. Communication between the processors is through the network on a peer-to-peer basis. Each user executes programs on his or her own local processor, using his or her own local memory. However, each user can use files on the shared file system that all users can access. The processor and memory on the server are used to manage the sharing of files and provide print services for a set of users. No individual's program is executed there; the only programs executing on the server manage the sharing of files and printers.

UNIX

A UNIX system has some features in common with the networked DOS system and some features that set it apart. In the UNIX

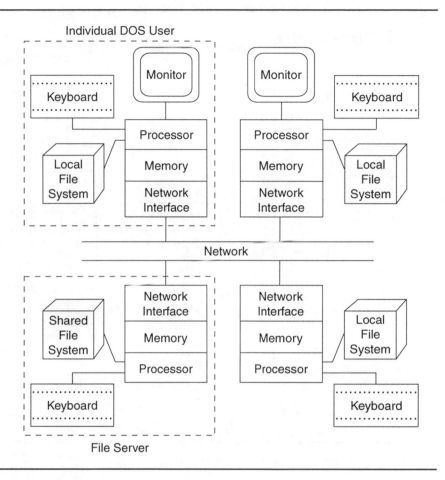

Figure 1.2.   Architectural view of networked DOS systems.

system as in the networked DOS case, files are shared among all users. In the networked DOS case, each user has a dedicated processor on which to execute programs; in the UNIX system all users execute programs on the same processor. As illustrated in Figure 1.3, all users must share not only the file system but the processor, too. In fact, users share the memory as well. Even though all users share the processor and the memory, the UNIX operating system isolates one user from another so that one user need not be aware of other users on the system. In this view of a UNIX system, users operate devices called *terminals* that are permanently attached to

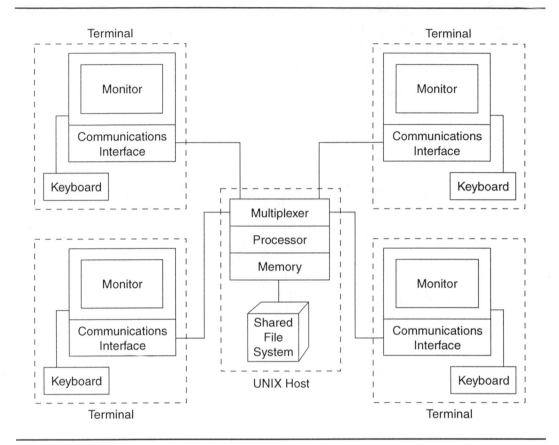

Figure 1.3.   Architectural view of UNIX system.

the UNIX system through terminal ports provided by a multiplexer. Terminals provide the user with an input/output device to use for interacting with the UNIX system but have no user-accessible memory or processor. Other methods of interacting with a UNIX system using the network are explored in chapter 13.

The UNIX operating system protects one user from another so that a user does not have to be conscious of the fact that he or she is sharing the processor with other users. This isolation is provided by the heart of the operating system, called the *kernel*. It is not necessary for the user to interface with the kernel of the operating system directly; UNIX instead provides a program, called

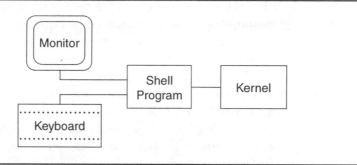

Figure 1.4.   UNIX system from user's point of view.

the *shell program*, to manage the user's interaction with the system. This shell program handles input from the keyboard and sends output to the monitor as illustrated in Figure 1.4. A user sees this shell program as his or her interface with the system and barely notices that there are other users on the very same system. This UNIX shell program is comparable to a DOS shell program in that the shell program provides its own commands to manage in which working directory the user is operating.

One area where the user is conscious of other users is the use of physical devices such as diskette drives and tape drives. On DOS systems, each individual system is dedicated to one user so that one user does not need to share any physical devices with any other user. But on UNIX systems, these devices must be shared with all users of the system. Thus, the diskette drives are always available to the DOS user but not to the UNIX user.

COMPARING DOS AND UNIX FEATURES

As discussed, the purposes of DOS and UNIX differ somewhat, but the method of attaining those goals has much in common. Many facets of DOS and UNIX are similar, while, of course, a number of areas differ. This section will compare the features of DOS and UNIX systems, followed by an examination of the differences between UNIX and DOS commands.

On both DOS and UNIX systems the directory structure is hierarchical, and navigation through the directory structure is the same. The concept of directories in which to gather files that belong together is the same for both DOS and UNIX. In addition, both systems provide special commands with which to create and destroy directories.

For both DOS and UNIX, a program manages the interaction of the keyboard with the processor. In DOS systems, it is usually **COMMAND.COM**; in UNIX systems it is a shell program as shown in Figure 1.4. Both of these programs bring their own commands with them and oversee the interaction of the user with the system.

On UNIX systems, no message will be given upon successful completion of a command. The DOS style is to notify the user of the successful completion of a command. For example, on DOS systems, when you copy files, the command will indicate how many files were copied. However, on UNIX systems, when you copy files, no message will be given, even if no files were actually copied, as long as the command syntax was correct. Historically, with much slower terminals on UNIX systems, providing positive feedback was not deemed very important.

As discussed earlier, only UNIX has multiple users accessing the system at the same time and running multiple programs. The only comparable DOS operation is multiple users accessing the same files on a file server. In UNIX, multiple programs are executing simultaneously; DOS does not really allow this, but other PC-based operating systems, such as OS/2 or Microsoft Windows, can run two programs simultaneously.

Users start a session on a UNIX system by logging in and identifying themselves to the system. DOS systems are just started up and no user identification is necessary. Networked DOS systems require that the user is identified to the system before accessing network facilities. In UNIX systems, once the user is identified, an environment customized to the particular user is set up. Different users will have different environments simultaneously. A DOS environment is the same, whichever user is using the system.

Naming conventions differ for UNIX and DOS. First, UNIX is case-sensitive; DOS is not. Thus, on UNIX systems, files named *AAA* and *aaa* are separate files; on DOS systems, there would only be one file. Second, on DOS systems, the period (.) is used to separate the *filename* (the characters to the left of the period) from the *extension* (the characters to the right of the period). On UNIX systems the period is just another character in a filename. For example, on UNIX systems, a period can begin the name of a file and appear twice or more in the name of a file, whereas on DOS systems, filenames cannot begin with a period, nor can they contain more than one period. Third, on DOS systems the characters to the right of the period indicate the kind of file. On UNIX systems, extensions have no special meaning. Finally, on DOS systems, a maximum of eight characters can be entered to the left of the period, and a maximum of three characters to the right. On UNIX systems, no limit exists on how many characters can be on either side of the period, but the total length of filenames is usually limited to 128 characters. In fact, names of files on UNIX systems do not have to have a period in them. In DOS systems, the name of a directory is limited to eight characters, while in UNIX systems the name of a directory is only limited to the maximum size of a filename.

In DOS, the directory name is separated from the filename with a back slash (\), while in UNIX the separation character performs the same function but is a forward slash (/). In DOS systems, the fully qualified name of a file shows the name of the physical drive containing that file, while in UNIX no physical drive specification is needed. Files on non-networked DOS systems have no owner or access control because the DOS system is dedicated to a single user. Files in UNIX systems have ownership and access control permissions just as in networked DOS systems, because these are shared file systems.

UNIX systems have a built-in facility so that commands can be scheduled to run periodically in the background (not attached to any terminal) while other processing occurs. DOS has no such scheduling nor any background facility.

COMPARING DOS AND UNIX COMMANDS

The UNIX style is for command names to be short to save typing, while the DOS style is for commands to have meaningful names. For example, the name of the command to copy files on a DOS system is **copy**, while for UNIX the same command is **cp**. The name of the file that performs a command in DOS must end in

.COM or .EXE, but in UNIX, a command may be any name and the file has the same name as the command.

For DOS systems, command line options are specified by the forward slash (/), while in UNIX systems, command line options are specified by the hyphen (-). In DOS systems, expansion of wildcard specifications (such as * or ?) is done by the command itself when it is executed. On UNIX systems, expansion of wildcard specifications is performed by the shell program before the command is executed, and the command sees just a list of files on which to operate.

The DOS operations of copying files, renaming files, deleting files, creating directories, and deleting directories have matching capabilities in UNIX systems. A comparison of these operations on both UNIX and DOS systems is found in Appendix B. Both operating systems have a range of commands to perform these functions. Usually the commands on the UNIX systems provide more options and a wider range of functions.

A scripting language is available on both DOS and UNIX systems. Script files that execute commands on a DOS system are called *batch files*, while on UNIX systems these files are called *shell scripts*. On both systems, these scripts are created using a text editor. Scripting facilities are quite a bit more extensive in UNIX than in DOS, but the concept is the same.

Output from DOS commands can be passed into other commands in an operation called a *pipe*. These pipeline operations are more generalized in UNIX than in DOS, although similar operations can be performed. Pipeline commands do not use temporary files in UNIX systems as they do in DOS systems; in fact, in UNIX every line of output is processed through the entire pipeline as it is created.

WHERE DOES UNIX COME FROM AND WHERE IS IT GOING?

UNIX was developed in the late 1960s by Ken Thompson and Dennis Ritchie of AT&T Bell Laboratories. The first version of UNIX was written in a machine language assembler, but was later rewritten in the C language in 1973. UNIX was made available to colleges and universities in 1974, and licenses were made widely available by AT&T in 1975. In 1979, the Computer Science Department at the University of California at Berkeley released its own version of UNIX, which contained many new features and is usually referred to as the BSD (Berkeley Software Distribution) version.

One advantage of the UNIX operating system over previous operating systems is that UNIX was made available on a large range of hardware platforms. This goal was accomplished by programming the UNIX operating system in the C language. Thus, hardware manufacturers could create versions of UNIX for their own hardware systems just by creating compilers for C that ran on their hardware. Individual vendors developed their UNIX offerings from the two versions mentioned earlier: the AT&T version, now known as System V, and the BSD software. Vendors were free to choose which features to offer from either of these two versions of UNIX. In addition, these UNIX vendors added programs from various sources to enrich and differentiate their offerings.

What this varied UNIX system lineage means for the user of UNIX is that a particular UNIX system will contain a core of programs, but, in addition, may contain any of a number of other programs. Further, the syntax for a particular program may differ from vendor to vendor. This book has concentrated on commands that will be found on all hardware platforms and has tried to use the syntax that is most commonly found on a range of hardware platforms.

Even today, development of UNIX systems has continued. New features are added to the UNIX systems to make them easier to administer, easier to network, and easier on which to run applications. Further, Novell, one of the main DOS networking companies, has purchased a UNIX system provider and has come out with its own version of UNIX for the personal computer. In addition, several new noncommercial UNIX systems for the personal computer, Linux and FreeBSD, have been developed that are available via the network and are free. Development of UNIX systems will continue as the need for UNIX-based computing resources to promote networking and client/server applications (see chapter 13) grows.

Starting and Ending User Sessions

OVERVIEW

UNIX systems, unlike DOS systems, were created to be multiuser. Because of this, the system needs to determine some information about who is attempting to use the system. In addition, the user environment can be tailored to the user, and thus, when the user is identified to the system, the user environment is created based on the identity of the user. This chapter begins by discussing how to start a user session, how to enter commands, and how to get help with a command. The chapter ends with a description of how to end user sessions.

STARTING A USER SESSION (LOGGING IN)

DOS systems are standalone systems managed by one individual user whose name is not important, while UNIX systems are designed to be shared among different users. To execute commands on a UNIX system, the user must first identify him- or herself to the system. This user identification process is called *logging in* and consists of telling the system of the name of the user. This process is quite foreign to standalone DOS systems. After the user has been identified to the system, the system will want to verify that this user is who he or she claims to be and will ask for a password to be entered. After the password has been entered and verified, the user is finally able to perform tasks on the UNIX system. This operation of identifying oneself to a system establishes a *user session* on this system for that user. This user session will continue until the user logs off and ends this user session.

The dialogue to log into a system begins when a user sits down at a terminal. The first message that greets that user is the request:

```
enter login:
```

What the user must do at this point is to enter his or her name. If the message **enter login:** is not displayed on the terminal, the user may have to press the **Enter** key once or twice to get the system to prompt you for your user name. The user name must be entered in the correct case because UNIX is case sensitive. Thus, the user *Alice* is different from the user *alice*. Usually your user name is assigned by the system administrator. The user name will be echoed back to the screen and the following will appear:

```
enter password:
```

Now the user enters his or her password, which will not be echoed to the screen. The system will then validate the user's name and password and, if all is proper, will start a terminal session for that user. If either an incorrect user name or password is entered, the user will be asked for his or her name and password a second time. After a third incorrect user name or password, the login session will be halted.

The instant that the system recognizes the user's name and password, the system will start a program to handle input from the user's terminal. In DOS, this program is usually the **COMMAND.COM** program, but in UNIX a shell program is usually used. The system administrator for the UNIX system will assign a shell program to a particular user. After the user's name and password are validated and accepted, the shell program has the user in its control. On UNIX systems, several different shell programs exist: the Bornshells, the Korn shell (named for its creator), and the C shell (named for its C language-like syntax). Each of these shell programs will create an environment that can be tailored to each individual user. If the user is using the Korn shell, one special file, the *.profile* file, is read and executed for the user when the user starts a terminal session. If the user is using the C shell, two special files, the *.login* and the *.cshrc* files, are read and executed in sequence. How these files are used and what they contain is discussed in some detail in chapters 9 and 10. For our purposes, we need only point out that these two files will be executed and then a *prompt* will appear at the user's terminal.

The process of logging in and starting a user session has an advantage for the user in that the environment of each logged-in user can be different while all users are sharing one UNIX system.

The name of a user must be registered on the system before that user can start a session on the UNIX system. This process of registration is usually performed by the UNIX system administrator. The directory in which the user is placed after logging in is usually called the *home directory*. This directory is defined for the user when the system administrator registers a user for that system. This directory will usually contain all of the files that a user creates.

On UNIX systems, not all users are equal. One particular user, the system administrator, performs many of the setup operations on the system. These functions are protected from the rest of the user community by requiring that only privileged users can perform these functions. These special users are called *root* or *superuser* and are special because they can change the attributes of any file and can perform any operation on the UNIX system. Like all other users, the root user has a password and must be logged in before any operations are performed.

ENTERING COMMANDS

Once login is completed and a prompt appears, the user can enter a command to tell the shell program what to do. Every time the prompt is displayed, the user may type in a new command. When a prompt does not appear, it usually means that the shell program is busy doing some other operation and cannot accept a command from the user at that time. Instructions on how to execute more than one command at a time are discussed in chapter 7.

All of the information entered at the prompt is called the *command line*. The first item that is entered (terminated by a blank) is assumed by the shell program to be the name of a command. Any items that are entered after the command itself are called *command line arguments*, and each of the arguments is separated by one or more blanks. On DOS systems, command options are entered next after the command and start with a forward slash (/). In UNIX systems command options are started with a hyphen (-), which must be entered just after the name of the command and before the command line arguments. All entries that follow the command and begin with a hyphen are considered command options until the first entry is found that does not begin with a hyphen. All entries after that will be considered to be command line arguments. For example, in DOS, to examine the contents of a directory one screenful at a time, you would enter the command

    dir/p

which requests the execution of the **dir** command with the command line option of **p**. On a UNIX system, you would enter the following command:

    ls -af

which requests the execution of the command **ls** to list the files in the current directory and specifies the command options as **af**. You could also specify the command options as separate entries as in

    ls -a -f

Just as in DOS, the order in which you specify the options does not matter. (Occasionally UNIX command options will not need the hyphen, but that is the exception.)

In DOS, to display the attributes of an individual file, you would use the command

    dir harry

while in UNIX you would enter the command

ls -aCF harry

which would request the execution of the **ls** command, would specify the command options as **aCF**, and the command line argument as **harry**. As indicated above, you cannot intersperse command options and command line arguments. The following command

ls -a -C harry -F

would request the execution of the **ls** command, would specify the command options as **aC**, and the command line arguments as **harry** and **-F**.

In UNIX just as in DOS, pushing the **Enter** key will terminate the command line and cause the shell program (or **COMMAND.COM**) to process what has been entered on the command line.

You can continue the command and its various arguments onto another line by ending the line with a back slash (****) and a carriage return. The next line will be started with a question mark (**?**) indicating that this is a continuation of the previous line.

Some Simple UNIX Commands

This section reviews some simple commands to familiarize you with the interaction with a UNIX system.

One simple command to try is the command to display the date and time that the system has, that is, the **date** command. On DOS systems, you would use two different commands, **DATE** and **TIME**, to display the date and time. Just as in DOS, the **date** command can be used to change the date and time on the system, but unlike DOS, the user would have to be privileged for the command to succeed on a UNIX system. The **date** command is executed by just entering it at the command line:

date

and the display generated will be

```
Mon Apr 11 14:07:21 EDT 1994
```

This command has a number of formatting options allowing the user to change the format of date and time that is shown. The format in which to display the current date is specified after a plus sign (**+**). To illustrate one formatting option, try the command

> **date +"%A %B %d, %Y at %r"**

and you will see displayed

```
Wednesday March 16, 1994 at 03:06:41 PM
```

which differs from the output without option displayed. Notice that in this case the command option was started with a plus sign (**+**) and not a dash (**-**). This is one of the few commands on a UNIX system that does not behave like all the others.

Changing either the date or the time has differing consequences for a DOS system or a UNIX system. On a DOS system, you will only affect one user if you change the date or time, but on a UNIX system, changing the date or the time affects all the users of the system. Because of the far-reaching consequences, changing the date or time is a privileged operation that can only be performed by the root user.

Another simple command to try is the **cal** command, which will display the calendar for a month and year. You can specify a month and year of interest, or if none is specified, the current month will be displayed (or previous, current, and next months are displayed). Thus, the command **cal** will display

```
         Oct                        Nov                        Dec
 S  M Tu  W Th  F  S        S  M Tu  W Th  F  S        S  M Tu  W Th  F  S
              1  2              1  2  3  4  5  6                 1  2  3  4
 3  4  5  6  7  8  9        7  8  9 10 11 12 13        5  6  7  8  9 10 11
10 11 12 13 14 15 16       14 15 16 17 18 19 20       12 13 14 15 16 17 18
17 18 19 20 21 22 23       21 22 23 24 25 26 27       19 20 21 22 23 24 25
24 25 26 27 28 29 30       28 29 30                   26 27 28 29 30 31
31
```

when the current date was a day in November, 1993. To display the calendar for the month of June in the year 1994, you would enter the command:

> **cal 6 1994**

which would display

```
            June 1994
    Sun Mon Tue Wed Thu Fri Sat
                 1   2   3   4
     5   6   7   8   9  10  11
    12  13  14  15  16  17  18
    19  20  21  22  23  24  25
    26  27  28  29  30
```

Another simple command displays the names of the other users on the system: the **who** command. Because only one user executes commands on a DOS system, there is no comparable DOS command. While the **who** command has a number of command line options, it can be entered without options as in

who

and the output that you receive will look like

```
    jsmith    pts/0   Nov 23 14:51   (178.128.112.112)
    marick    pts/3   Nov 23 14:53   (178.128.112.156)
    mjones    pts/7   Nov 23 15:35   (goofy.what.com)
    jwilson   pts/8   Nov 23 15:37   (goofy.what.com)
```

which shows that there are four users on the system. The display generated by the **who** command may differ somewhat from UNIX system to UNIX system.

Another use of the **who** command is to determine your user name by adding the option **am i**, as in the following example:

who am i

which will display something like

```
    marick    ttyp0       Nov 22 15:25
```

which indicates that you are "marick" on the terminal port "ttyp0" and you logged in at "Nov 22 15:25."

Another way to look at the activity on the system is to use the **w** command (which is not available on every system), which will list users on the system and what commands they are doing. As an example, output from the **w** command is shown in Table 2.1,

Table 2.1.   Output from the **w** Command

```
03:15PM  up 1 day, 15:57, 14 users, load average: 0.59,0.43,0.35
    User     tty       login@   idle   JCPU   PCPU   what
    jsmith   pts/0     02:02PM   1:12      0      0   -csh
    marick   pts/3     02:49PM      0     10     10   trn
    bharris  pts/6     12:24PM      3     13      2   trn
    jwilson  pts/8     10:09AM      1     17     17   vi
    hgoode   pts/12    Thu10AM      0     39      2   -ksh
```

which indicates that the system has not been restarted for more than one day and 15 hours, that there are 14 users currently on the system, and that the load on the system is less than one (that is to say, not very busy). For each user, the port address, the time they logged in, how long they have been idle, and what command they are currently executing are displayed. Only some selected lines of the command output are shown.

The help **Command**

DOS systems provide a **help** command to enable the user to find some information about a command. UNIX systems also provide an extensive system of help for individual commands, which works on two levels. The first level is provided by the individual command itself. If you enter a command but specify an incorrect option, the command will reply with a message indicating that an unrecognized option was specified, and in addition, will display messages indicating just what the proper options are. For example, the **ls** command will display several lines of messages if an incorrect option is chosen. Thus, if you enter the command

    ls -z jerry

the **ls** command will display

```
ls: illegal option - z
usage: ls [ -1ACFLRabcdfgilmnopqrstux ] [files]
```

which indicates that **z** is not a proper option, but any of **1ACF ...** is. These explanations of correct command usage do not show what any of the options do, only what the available options are. These messages are only useful if you know what the command does but you cannot remember which option to use.

To find out what a command and each of its options really do, you would read the "manual page" for that command. To read a manual page at a terminal, you would enter the **man** command and specify the name of the command that you are interested in. For example, the command

man ls

would provide many screens full of information describing in detail how the **ls** command works and how each of the options of the **ls** command operates. The manual page for a command is divided into sections to make it easier to find the kind of information you are seeking. All of the individual options for a command are shown first and the description of each of the options is found later in the manual page. Unfortunately, unlike the DOS facility of **help**, if you don't know the name of the command you are looking for, you will not be able to use the **man** command, because it will only display the manual page for the command that you specify. No command browsing facility is available to make finding the correct command name easier. Toward the end of a manual page describing a particular command, a *See Also* section will indicate which commands are associated with the command currently being examined. This section is useful to help you figure out the name of a command in which you are interested but do not know the exact name.

To examine all the functionality that the **date** command provides, display the manual page that describes the functionality of the **date** command by entering the command

man date

which will display text describing how to use the **date** command.

ENDING A USER SESSION (LOGGING OUT)

After you have done all that you wish while you are logged into the host, you can end the user session or *log out*. On a DOS system, a user would probably just turn off the system, but since the system is used by multiple users, a UNIX system is never turned off. Depending on which shell program you are running, you can log out by entering the **logout** command (for the Korn shell) or by entering **exit** command (for the Korn shell or C shell). Once you have ended your user session, you will see the prompt:

```
enter login:
```

appear again as at the beginning of your user session. Now someone else could use this same terminal and log in as another user.

When you log out, if you have jobs running in the background (see chapter 7 for a discussion of background jobs), these jobs will continue to run if there is no output or input pending. Any jobs that have been suspended will be ended. If there are jobs pending, you will be warned with the message:

```
Suspended jobs pending
```

before you will be able to log out.

HOW USER NAMES AND PASSWORDS ARE CONSTRUCTED

User names must be unique in a UNIX system, but there can be multiple user sessions under the same user name. User names are from three to eight characters long, start with a letter, and can contain numbers. They are case sensitive as is most of UNIX. Thus, the following are valid and different user names:

```
marick
mra
Marick
mArick2
m22
```

Names like "mra" and "m22" are usually allowed but should not be used because they are too short. But names like the following

```
11111
m_44444
```

are not usually valid. Often an institution such as a university or a company will have a standard way of constructing user names. One choice is to use a person's initials, or first name followed by enough letters in the last name to create a unique user name. One other common scheme is to use the first letter of the first name and the first seven letters of the last name. Passwords can contain an underline (_) and even a caret (^). Special characters are a good way of creating a difficult-to-decipher password. Often when a user is first defined on a system, the person who defines the user will assign a standard password and the user will be required to change his or her password when first logging in. On some systems the user can be forced to change the password when starting his or her first session on a host.

A user can change his or her password at any time by using the **passwd** command. Entering the command

passwd

will cause the following message to appear

```
Setting password for user: marty
```

and to make sure that the user changing the password is the real user, the current password is prompted with the message

```
Old password:
```

to which the user would enter the current password, which will not be echoed. If what you entered is correct, you will get messages that are similar to

```
Last successful password change for marty:
        Fri Jul 23 17:42:14 1993
Last unsuccessful password change for marty:
        Tue Nov 30 09:45:29 1993

Choose password

You can pick a password.
```

followed by the message requesting that you enter the new password

```
Please enter new password (at least 3 characters):
```

to which you would reply with a new password. This changed password will be verified by requesting that you give the changed password a second time with the message

```
Re-enter password:
```

to which you would reply with the changed password. If the two matched, the password would be changed to the new one that you requested.

New passwords are validated to ensure that the password chosen is hard to guess, unique, and not the same as the previous password. For example, the new password must be at least six characters long and on many systems must contain at least one number or one upper-case character. If the new password that you have chosen does not follow the rules for choosing new passwords, it will be rejected and the password will stay the same. Some possible rejection messages are

```
You may not reuse the same password.

Sorry, password not acceptable:
    Passwords must differ by at least three positions.

Sorry, password not acceptable:
    Must contain at least two alphabetic characters
    and at least one numeric or special character.
```

If you fail to choose an acceptable new password in three attempts, the **passwd** command will halt execution and return you to the command line.

THE ROLE OF THE SUPERUSER

On a multiuser UNIX system, every user (except for one) is equal. But some operations, such as defining new users or reconfiguring the system, require a privileged status for a user. This special user is called the superuser or root. All the operations dealing with managing the system can only be done by the superuser.

For example, the superuser can change a normal user's password. Also, the superuser does not know any user's current password. In addition, the superuser can modify the permissions and ownership of any directory or file. Because of these capabilities, the password for the superuser is carefully guarded. Usually one person is designated the system administrator for a computer and that person knows the password for the superuser.

Exercises

The following is a short exercise on a UNIX system to try out starting up and ending a user session and executing some simple commands.

1. Login to a UNIX system. What command did you use?
2. Determine which shell you are running.
3. Enter the **date** command.
4. Try to execute the **date** command but misspell "date" and enter **dtae** instead. What error message did you get? Why did you get that message and not "Misspelled Command"?
5. Examine the manual page for the **date** command. What command did you use to do that?
6. Examine the manual page for the **who** command.
7. Determine who is logged into the system. Is anybody logged on more than once? Is that possible? Are you shown on this list?
8. Use the **who** command to find out who you are. How much CPU time has your logon process used? How do you know that?
9. List current users, showing the state of their terminal, activity, and PID number. Display only the names and number of users. What command did you use? Have any users been idle for a long time? Why would that happen?
10. Change your password. What command did you use to accomplish that?
11. End your user session. What command did you use?
12. Now log back into the system using the new password. Is there any record of the commands that you entered in the previous user session?

UNIX File System

OVERVIEW

To work with a file, it is necessary to know how to name that file. This chapter will introduce the UNIX file system and the concepts of filenames, directories, and subdirectories. These file system methods are similar to DOS file system methods. In addition, the naming of files using relative names and the idea of a "current working directory" are introduced. How to change your current working directory and how to display the contents of a directory are also discussed. The idea of file attributes such as ownership and access permission is introduced. Finally, commands to determine the available disk space will be discussed.

WHAT IS A DIRECTORY?

A typical DOS or UNIX computer system has many files just as a business has many files. Just as a business has file drawers in a file cabinet to organize files into groups, both DOS and UNIX provide *directories* to organize files into groups.

Just as a business has several file cabinets to further segment groups of files, DOS and UNIX allow directories to be hierarchically organized. Thus, directories can contain not only files but other directories. A directory within another directory is called a *subdirectory*. In a UNIX system, unlike a DOS system, user files are usually organized by the user that owns them. On UNIX systems, the system files are organized by their functions. A typical UNIX file system is illustrated in Figure 3.1, where each directory has a box around it and each file has no box. Thus, in this picture *bin*, *dev*, *etc*, *lib*, *tmp*, and *usr* are all the names of directories. Within the *u* directory there are two more directories: *john* and *marty*. In this figure, only one directory, *marty*,

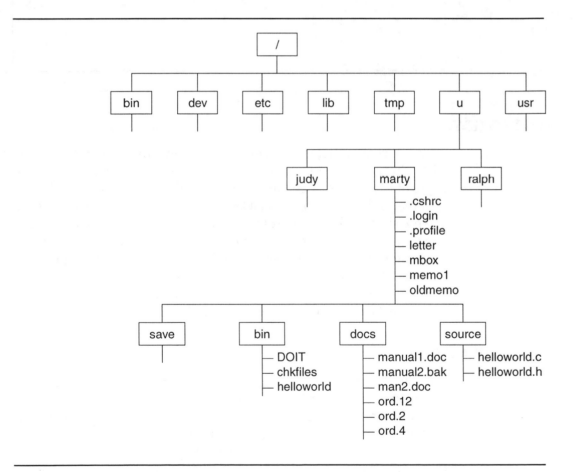

Figure 3.1.   Layout of directories and files in a typical UNIX system.

contains both directories and files. The directory hierarchy can contain several more levels if the user wishes. The top level directory (/) is usually called the *root* directory and contains both directories and files used by the operating system.

HOW ARE FILES NAMED?

Every file in a UNIX or DOS file system has a name by which it is identified in commands. Each level in the directory structure is referred to by putting a "/" in front of the name of the level, except for the root directory. In DOS file systems, files are located on different drives; to specify fully the name of a file you must specify which drive the file resides on. UNIX systems do not require drive specification, even if there are several physical drives on your system. The existence of multiple physical or logical drives is hidden from you on UNIX systems. For example, the full name of a file in DOS might be **C:\REPORTS\MAY10.DAT**. But in UNIX, no drive designation is necessary, even if there is more than one disk drive on the system. The file would be called **/reports/may10.dat** in UNIX.

On UNIX systems, files and directories can be named almost anything. Names can begin with letters (both upper and lowercase), numbers, period (.), and even underscore (_). Unlike DOS systems, both directory and file names are case sensitive; thus, "a" is the name of one file while "A" would be the name of another file. While the maximum length of a file name is twelve characters on a DOS system, the maximum length of a file or directory name that all UNIX systems support is fourteen characters, although most systems support much longer names. Unlike in DOS systems, the period (.) is not a special character in the naming of UNIX files. For example, ".a.a.a.a." is a valid file name in a UNIX system but not in a DOS system, as are such names as

```
1
1aa
.1aa
_1.a
_a
_A
```

When picking filenames, use those that are representative of the function of the file and are easy to type. The file name "AaBbCc" is valid but a problem to type.

For both DOS and UNIX systems, the root directory is referred to by "\" (DOS) or "/" (UNIX) alone. The *u* directory would be referred to by "\u (DOS) or "/u" (UNIX). A file is referred to in the same way as a directory. Thus, the file *memo1* in the *marty* directory in the *u* directory would have a full filename in DOS systems of:

```
C:\u\marty\memo1
```

while in UNIX systems it would be

```
/u/marty/memo1
```

As another example, the file *manual1* in a lower-level directory *docs* would have the full filename in DOS of

```
C:\u\marty\docs\manual1
```

while in UNIX the full filename would be

```
/u/marty/docs/manual1
```

Specifying the full name of a file every time you need to refer to it would seem to be a cumbersome requirement, so both DOS and UNIX allow "relative" file naming by assuming that any file or directory name that does not start with a "/" is the name of a file or directory relative to the directory in which you are currently working. Thus, if you need to operate on files in the *marty* directory, instead of referring to them by preceding each name with */u/marty*, UNIX allows the user to operate in the */u/marty* directory and refer to the files just by name. The simple rule of relativity is that when the name of a file starts with a "/", that name must be the full pathname and when it does not start with a "/", that name is relative to the directory where the user is currently working. For example, referring to a file as *memo1* would indicate a file that is in the current directory; referring to a file as *marty/memo1* would indicate a file *memo1* that is in the subdirectory *marty* relative to the current directory, and referring to a file as */u/marty/memo1* would indicate a file in the */u/marty* directory, regardless of the current directory.

DISPLAYING YOUR CURRENT WORKING DIRECTORY

The current working directory is the directory in which the system will start to look for a file that is relatively named on which you wish to perform some operation. The initial current working directory that you are in when you start a user session is usually set up for the user by the administrator of the system. The first command that many users learn is the one that shows the user what directory the user is currently working in, and the **pwd** command accomplishes that. On DOS systems the command **cd** performs this same function; on UNIX systems the command **cd** by itself causes a change in the directory to the home directory of the user. Thus, if you enter the UNIX command **pwd**, the system will display at your terminal:

```
/u/marty
```

if your current working directory is */u/marty*; the DOS command **cd** command would display

```
C:\u\marty
```

For example, if you wanted to copy one file to another, the system would look in the current working directory for the file to copy. If the file did not exist, you would receive the message "File not found."

CHANGING YOUR CURRENT WORKING DIRECTORY

The next important command tells the system to change the user's current working directory to a different directory. The **cd** command, which is the same in both UNIX and DOS, is followed by the name of the directory that the user would like to use as the current working directory. DOS provides a second command, **chdir**, to do the same operation but UNIX does not. If such a directory exists, the shell program will now set the current working directory to the new requested one. If such a directory does not exist, an error message will be displayed, usually something like:

```
file or directory doesn't exist
```

and the current directory is not changed. Thus, the DOS command:

> **cd c:\usr\lib**

will change your working directory to *\usr\lib*. The UNIX command

> **cd /usr/lib**

will change your working directory to */usr/lib*. As another example, the command:

> **cd /usr/spool/lp/interface**

will change your working directory to */usr/spool/lp/interface*. Any reference to a file or a directory that begins with a leading "/" is a fully qualified filename or a full pathname.

You can use a relative directory reference to indicate what directory you wish to change to. Thus, if your current working directory was */u/fred* and you entered the command:

> **cd source**

the system would try to change to the *source* directory relative to the directory in which you are currently. Any time a directory is specified without a "/", the shell program assumes this is a directory relative to your current working directory. Thus, **cd source** is equivalent to the command:

> **cd//u/fred/source**

and both would set the current working directory to the same directory, */u/fred/source*, if the directory exists.

You can also change to a directory that is in the same hierarchy as the current working directory but may not be a subdirectory of the current working directory. For example, suppose that in the directory */u/fred* there are two subdirectories, *source* and *bin*. If your current working directory is */u/fred/source*, how would you change to the directory */u/fred/bin*? Obviously, the following command would work:

cd /u/fred/bin

but there is a shorter command to specify the directory you want without specifying its absolute path. You could instead specify a relative directory path by the following command:

cd ../bin

which means move up into the next higher directory and then down into the subdirectory *bin*. If you specify the command:

cd ..

you will move up one level in the directory hierarchy. You can move up in the directory hierarchy as many levels as you need to by adding more "../" specifications in the **cd** command. Thus, if you were in the directory */u/fred/bin* and you wanted to move to the directory */u/marty/source*, you could use the command:

cd ../../marty/source

which would mean move up two levels in the hierarchy and then down two levels to the directory of interest. Always the goal is to use whatever information the shell knows to make shorter the command that you enter at the terminal.

The home directory of a user is a special directory and can be reentered by just using the command **cd** without any other command line arguments. The home directory for a user is the directory in which you are immediately after you start your user session. Thus, the command

cd

by itself would return you to your home directory. In addition, the home directory for another user can be specified by a tilde (~) plus the name of the user and is always defined if that user has been defined on that system. If the tilde is followed by a string of characters, the string of characters is assumed to be the name of a user and the home directory of that user will be substituted for the tilde and the string. For example, the command:

cd ~harry

would change the working directory to the home directory of the user named *harry*. The user's home directory is assigned by the system administrator. As another example, the command:

cd ~harry/programs

would change the working directory to a subdirectory in the home directory of the user *harry*. Notice that in using this notation, you do not need to know the home directory of the user *harry*.

On some systems, if the name of the directory that you have specified does not exist but a similarly named directory does, the UNIX system will ask you whether this is the name of the directory that you wanted. For example, on a SCO UNIX system, if a directory named *source1* existed and you specified the command:

cd source

which did not exist, the system will prompt with the message:

```
source1 ok?
```

You can accept this choice by hitting the **Enter** key. Other UNIX systems may have ways to request the system to fill in the name of the directory that you want when you only know the first few letters.

LISTING THE CONTENTS OF DIRECTORIES

Once you have arrived in a particular directory, you will want to find out what files are contained within this directory. On a DOS system, you would use the **dir** command as in:

dir

which would display all of the files in that directory. On a UNIX system, you would use the **ls** command; For example, if you issued the command:

ls

a list of the files in the current directory would be listed, either in one column or in five columns (depending on UNIX system) in alphabetical order with uppercase filenames first. Usually filenames and directory names in UNIX systems are lowercase letters, but that is not a necessary condition. On a UNIX system the **ls** command without any options will only list the files in the directory, while on a DOS system, the **dir** command will list not only the names of the files but also their size and date of last modification. For example, on a DOS system, if you were in the *c:\u\marty* directory and issued the **dir** command (see Figure 3.1), you would see output similar to that shown in Figure 3.2, which indicates that *bin*, *docs*, *save*, and *source* are directories while the others are files. This command even indicates the amount of free space on your system.

On the other hand, on a UNIX system, if you were in the */u/marty* directory and issued the **ls** command (see Figure 3.1), you would see output similar to that in Figure 3.3, which does not indicate that *bin*, *docs*, *save* and *source* are directories while the others are files, nor does it indicate how much free space is available.

In order to display which files are directories and which are not, you use the command line option **F**, which will indicate whether an object in a directory is a file or a subdirectory. Thus, executing the command:

ls -F

```
Volume in drive C is MS-DOS_5
Volume Serial Number is 10FE-0749
Directory of C:\USR\MARTY

BIN            <DIR>          07-16-94     9:48p
DOCS           <DIR>          07-18-94     8:48a
LETTER                15,328  05-04-94     7:16p
MBOX                   3,456  03-04-94     3:06p
MEMO1                 23,148  02-04-94     8:06p
OLDMEMO               21,348  01-04-94     9:06p
SAVE           <DIR>          06-26-94     3:48p
SOURCE         <DIR>          06-26-94     3:48p

5 File(s)         38,476 bytes
            13,705,216 bytes free
```

Figure 3.2.   Output from **dir** command on DOS system.

```
bin
docs
letter
mbox
memo1
oldmemo
save
source
```

Figure 3.3.   Output from **ls** command on DOS system.

would cause the following to display on your terminal:

```
bin/
docs/
letter
mbox
memo1
oldmemo
save/
source/
```

Notice that the directories are marked with a forward slash (/) at the end of their names. Executable files will have an asterisk (*) after their names.

Notice that you did not specify any particular files for which to display the attributes. The default for the **ls** command is to display all of the files (except for the ones that start with a period) in the current directory. If you want to limit what files are listed, you must specify the files in which you are interested. You can specify on the command line several files to list or several sets of criteria for which files to list. For example, the command

ls docs/ord* memo1 bin/DO*

would produce output that looks like

```
bin/DOIT
docs/ord.12
docs/ord.2
docs/ord.4
memo1
```

The asterisk (*) is a wildcard operator recognized by shell programs to mean "all character strings of any length." Thus, in our example above, **ord*** would match any files that start with **ord**. On DOS systems you would code "*.*" to represent all files in a directory; on UNIX systems this would only pick out the files that have an embedded period (.) in them. Thus, on a UNIX system you would use the asterisk by itself to represent all files.

On many UNIX systems by default the names of the files are listed in a single column to the left side of your terminal. When there are more than 24 files in your directory, some of the names of the files will roll off of the screen before you can read them. You can request that the listing be shown in columns by adding the "C" option. Now if you issued the command

ls -CF

you would see the output

```
bin/    docs/  letter  mbox  memo1
oldmemo save/  source/
```

which has put the filenames in a maximum of five columns.

The UNIX system maintains a number of pieces of information about a file. You can examine this information using the **l** (long) option. If you issue the command

ls -l memo1

you would see output that looks like Figure 3.4. In this listing you will find the name of the owner, the name of the group that owns the file, the size of the file, the read/write permissions of the file (access permissions for a file are discussed in a later chapter), and the date this file or directory was last modified. If you wanted to see the entire contents of a directory you could use the command

ls -l /u/marty

which would display Figure 3.5 on your terminal.

Another useful way to examine a directory is to look for the more recently modified files. The default listing that the **ls** command generates is alphabetized by file and directory name. You can display a set of files in reverse order of their modification

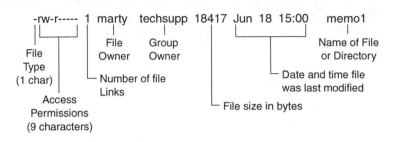

Figure 3.4.   Contents of long listing for a file.

date by using the **-t** option. Usually you want to see everything about a file so you would specify a command like

ls -tl

and you would see the output in Figure 3.6 for the */u/marty* directory.

Files that start with a period are considered hidden because the **ls** command will not display them if special option **-a** is not specified to request that these files be displayed. Figures 3.5 and 3.6 do not show all of the files in the */u/marty* directory. If you added the option to request that every file, including those that begin with a period, be displayed as in the command

ls -al /u/marty

```
total 30
drwx------   3 marty    sys         1880 Oct 16 14:03 bin
drwx------   3 marty    sys          880 Oct 12 18:01 docs
-rw-------   1 marty    sys         1795 Oct 15 20:05 letter
-rw-------   1 marty    sys          395 Oct 21 14:56 mbox
-rw-r--r--   1 marty    techsupp    6011 Sep 29 11:29 memo1
-rw-r-----   1 marty    techsupp    5185 Oct 21 12:48 oldmemo
drwx------   2 marty    sys          512 Oct 11 18:48 save
drwx------   2 marty    sys          768 Oct 21 13:58 scripts
```

Figure 3.5.   Contents of */u/marty* directory.

```
total 30
-rw-r--r--  1 marty    techsupp    6011 Sep 29 11:29 memo1
drwx------  2 marty    sys          512 Oct 11 18:48 save
drwx------  3 marty    sys          880 Oct 12 18:01 docs
-rw-------  1 marty    sys         1795 Oct 15 20:05 letter
drwx------  3 marty    sys         1880 Oct 16 14:03 bin
-rw-r-----  1 marty    techsupp    5185 Oct 21 12:48 oldmemo
drwx------  2 marty    sys          768 Oct 21 13:58 scripts
-rw-------  1 marty    sys          395 Oct 21 14:56 mbox
```

Figure 3.6.   Contents of directory ordered by modification date.

you would see the output as shown in Figure 3.7. Notice that there are quite a few files that begin with a period. These files are usually application startup files or application configuration files.

Directories have attributes similar to files. Notice the entry for the directory *scripts* in Figure 3.5. All of the column entries match those of a file as described in Figure 3.4. You can display the attributes of a directory by itself by using the command **ls -ld**. Thus, the command

> **ls -ld /u/marty**

```
total 50
drwx------   7 marty    techsupp     544 Oct 25 11:16 .
drwxrwxrwx  15 root     root         320 Oct 25 11:07 ..
-rw-------   1 marty    sys            6 Oct 13 13:40 .cshrc
-rw-------   1 marty    sys          116 Oct 13 13:41 .login
-rw-------   1 root     other        386 Oct 18 12:10 .profile
drwx------   3 marty    sys         1880 Oct 16 14:03 bin
drwx------   3 marty    sys          880 Oct 12 18:01 docs
-rw-------   1 marty    sys         1795 Oct 15 20:05 letter
-rw-------   1 marty    sys          395 Oct 21 14:56 mbox
-rw-r--r--   1 marty    techsupp    6011 Sep 29 11:29 memo1
-rw-r-----   1 marty    techsupp    5185 Oct 21 12:48 oldmemo
drwx------   2 marty    sys          512 Oct 11 18:48 save
drwx------   2 marty    sys          768 Oct 21 13:58 scripts
```

Figure 3.7.   Full contents of */u/marty* directory.

would display only the attributes of the directory */u/marty* itself
as in

```
drwx------ 7 marty sys 544 Oct 25 11:16
```

and would not display any of the contents of the directory. One
note of caution, the same command shown above without the **-d**
option would display the contents and not the attributes of the
/u/marty directory.

DETERMINING THE AMOUNT OF AVAILABLE DISK SPACE

Before you create very large files, you should determine that you
have disk space available for the file that you will be creating. On
DOS systems, you would use the **dir** command. On UNIX systems, you would use the **df** command. As an example, if you were
to execute the **df** command without arguments you might see
output similar to Figure 3.7.

The output from the **df** command that is displayed on your
terminal may differ somewhat from Figure 3.7 because different
UNIX systems offer different information about file systems. For
example, in a SCO UNIX system, the command

df -t

would produce output like

```
/   (/dev/root):   16730 blocks   28974 i-nodes
          total:  299980 blocks   37504 i-nodes
/u  (/dev/u   ):   29574 blocks   22716 i-nodes
          total:  190190 blocks   23776 i-nodes
```

which indicates there are two file systems on this system (/ and
/u). The command

df

would produce output like

```
/   (/dev/root):   16730 blocks   28974 i-nodes
/u  (/dev/u   ):   29574 blocks   22716 i-nodes
```

A block on a UNIX system is usually 512 bytes in length. Each file requires one i-node, and thus, the number of available i-nodes is the maximum number of files that can be created on that device.

The command

df -t ~

would produce output like

```
/u/martya  (/dev/u ):   29574 blocks  22716 i-nodes
              total:  190190 blocks  23776 i-nodes
```

which indicates that the partition for your home directory has 29574 blocks available.

The list of file systems shown in Figure 3.8 contains several that are not physically on the system on which this command was run. How such a file system is created is discussed in chapter 14. These file systems can be recognized by the fact that their name contains a colon (:). The designation to the left of the colon is the name of the system on which these file systems will be found, and the directory shown to the right of the colon is the directory where that file system is found. The name on the right side of the display is the name by which these file systems are known on this system. The names do not have to be similar, but

Filesystem	Total KB	used	free	%used	iused	ifree	%iused	Mounted on
/dev/hd1	4096	1076	3020	26%	66	958	6%	/home
/dev/hd2	151552	141684	9868	93%	9546	29366	24%	/usr
/dev/hd3	8192	300	7892	3%	19	2029	0%	/tmp
/dev/hd4	4096	3784	312	92%	717	307	70%	/
/dev/hd9var	4096	876	3220	21%	113	911	11%	/var
goofy:/goofy/docs	524288	515648	8640	98%	-	-	-	/goofy/docs
goofy:/goofy/pics	380928	333088	47840	87%	-	-	-	/goofy/pics
goofy:/usr/local	380928	303020	77908	79%	-	-	-	/usr/local

Figure 3.8.   Sample output from **df** command.

the system administrator will find managing these file systems difficult if the names are not quite similar. For those file systems physically on this processor, the directory names on the right of the display indicate how the file systems are named. File systems are often created so that if one file system runs out of disk space, the other parts of the system are not affected.

UNIX DIRECTORY STRUCTURE

Many directories will exist on any given DOS or UNIX system, but certain directories in a UNIX system will contain particular files to perform special functions. Many of these files are needed for the proper operation of the UNIX system, while other directories are just "file cabinets" containing a common set of commands or files. DOS systems do not necessarily have such directories. Some of these directories were shown in Figure 3.1. and their contents are as follows:

/ (root) Directory

The top directory in the UNIX file system is called the root directory and is designated by a forward slash (/). This master directory contains mostly other subdirectories and only a few files, mainly the executable file called **unix**, which is run to start the system. This directory normally contains a backup version of the **unix** file, which may be called something like **unix.old** or **unix.bak.** Few other files will be found in this directory. In DOS systems this directory contains *autoexec.bat*, *config.sys*, and other system files.

/bin Directory

The most frequently used UNIX system programs are found in the **bin** directory, which is short for "binary," another name for compiled executables.

/dev Directory

Special files representing peripheral devices (and some imaginary or "pseudo" devices) are found in this directory. These files represent devices of various types and use the same interface as ordinary files. Many commands will operate on these files in a similar fashion to regular files. Device handlers intercept read or write requests to these special files and process them accordingly, but users would not observe that behavior.

/etc Directory

This directory contains administrative and configuration programs and files. Many of the basic system commands that start up the system and start the various subsystems that manage such facilities as printing, networking, running jobs when scheduled, are found here.

/lib Directory

The system libraries used by various programs are contained here.

/tmp Directory

Temporary files created by various system utility programs are stored in this directory. Users can put files in this directory, too, but users should be aware that this directory is erased regularly.

/u Directory

Home directories for users are often contained within this directory, but this is not a UNIX system requirement. The person who sets up the system (called the system administrator) will usually designate at least one high-level directory that will contain all of the home directories for users of this system. On some UNIX systems, the **/home** directory contains user files.

/usr Directory

Files used by many of the system applications, such as the mail spooler and the printer spooler, will be found in this directory. Usually there is a directory, often called **/usr/local**, that contains commands that are installed on this system by the local system administrator. In addition, this same directory is often used by applications to store various files or subdirectories that an application might need.

Exercises

To work on your skill in navigating directories and examining files, you should do the following:

1. Start a user session on a UNIX system. How did you do that?
2. Determine your home directory and record its name. What command did you use to do that? Does this directory have a special significance? How does this directory get set up?
3. List the contents of this directory. What command did you use? Did you find any files there? Are you sure? If you found any files there, can you identify their uses? Did you list all of the contents of this directory?
4. Do you have any directories in your home directory? How do you know?
5. Make /bin your working directory. What command did you do to accomplish that?
6. Use the **ls** command to look at the files in this directory. Are there many files in this directory? Use an **ls** command to list the contents of this directory in columns. Do you recognize any of the objects in this directory?
7. Return to your home directory. What command did you use?
8. Make /dev your working directory. Examine what files are there. Do you recognize any of these files?
9. Return to your home directory.
10. Execute the **df** command on your system. Is all of that disk space physically on your local UNIX system? How could you tell? How much disk space is available to you? Is some free space not available to you?

Managing Files and Directories

OVERVIEW

The prior chapter focused on what the UNIX file system looks like. This chapter focuses on how to work with files and directories, including how to create them, how to copy them, and how to change their names. One difference between UNIX and DOS is in how to name a file or a directory. DOS has relatively strict naming conventions while UNIX has few. One section of this chapter tells how to name both directories and files. Both DOS and UNIX file systems can contain many files, even hundreds. Finding a particular file can require some serious detective work. One section in this chapter shows how to determine what directory a file is in. This chapter also discusses a particular UNIX function: limiting access to files and directories. The meaning of file and directory attributes and how to change them are explored.

Commands to determine the type of contents of a file will be discussed. Finally, the chapter will conclude by illustrating a command to create an alias name for a file or a directory.

CREATING FILES AND DIRECTORIES

To copy a file to another in DOS, you would use the **copy** command. For example, to copy a file *manual1.doc* from the *docs* directory to the *save* directory, you would issue the command

> **copy manual1.doc ..\save\manual1.doc**

In UNIX you would perform the same operation with the command

> **cp manual1.doc ../save/manual1.doc**

which will create a copy of the file *manual1.doc* in another directory, the *save* directory. If *manual1.doc* already exists, it will be overwritten. If the last argument on the command line is a directory, the files are copied into the directory. Thus, the command

> **cp manual1.doc man2.doc ../save**

will copy the files *manual1.doc* and *man2.doc* into the directory *save*. You can use wildcard characters to specify which files will be copied into the target directory. Thus, the command

> **cp man* ord.2 ../save**

will copy all files whose names begin with *man* into the directory *save* as well *ord.2*. To copy the contents of one directory into another, you would use a command like

> **cp marty/* newdir**

which will copy all of the files (except ones that begin with a period such as *.cshrc*) from directory *marty* into directory *newdir*. Notice the use of an asterisk to refer to all of the files that do not begin with a period. In DOS you would use the expression "*.*" to refer to all of the files in a directory, but in UNIX systems, the period is just another letter in a file name. Thus, in UNIX systems, the expression "*.*" refers to files that have a period in their names such as *manual1.doc* and excludes files such as *letter* that do not have a period in their name.

If you wish to copy files into the current directory, you use the period to refer to the current directory. For example, the command

> **cp olddir/* .**

which will copy the files from the directory *olddir* into the current directory.

In DOS systems, you can use the **copy** command to combine files. In UNIX systems you cannot use the **cp** command to combine files, you must use the **cat** command instead. For example, in DOS systems, you would use the command

copy ord.12+ord.2+ord.4 ord.all

to create the file *ord.all* that would contain the *ord.12*, *ord.2*, and *ord.4* files. On UNIX systems, the **cat** command is used to concatenate files. Thus, you specify which files are to be combined and the **cat** command will write them to standard output. You would use redirection to write these files into a new file that contains the contents of all the files. Redirecting output to a file in UNIX is just like in DOS systems and even uses the same operator, the greater than sign (>). Thus, the command

cat ord.12 ord.2 ord.4

will write the contents of these files in succession onto your display screen. If you wanted to combine them into one file, you would add redirection to the end of the command (just as in DOS). Thus, you would change the above command to be

cat ord.12 ord.2 ord.4 > ord.all

which would write the contents of these files in succession into the file *ord.all*.

Directories are special kinds of files and thus require special commands to create and remove them. Just like DOS, the command **mkdir** is used to create directories in UNIX and the command **rmdir** is used to delete a directory. But, unlike DOS, there is no standard alias for **mkdir** or **rmdir**. Thus, in DOS the command to create the directory *backup* is

md c:\backup

while in UNIX the command would be

mkdir /backup

would create the *backup* directory. Once a directory has been created, it can be used immediately to store files. In DOS systems, you examine the contents of a directory with the command

dir c:\backup

while in UNIX you would use the command

ls /backup

You can examine the definition of the directory itself with the command

ls -ld /backup

which would produce output something like

```
drwxrwxrwx 1 martya support 1024 Jun 18 5:00 backup
```

indicating that any user of the system can define files in the directory *backup*.

To change the name of a file, in UNIX you would use the **mv** command ("move"). For example, to rename the file *goodstuff* as the file *betterstuff*, in DOS you would use the command

rename goodstuff betterstuff

but on a UNIX system, you would execute the command

mv goodstuff betterstuff

which looks very much the same except for the use of a different command.

To change the name of a directory, in UNIX systems you would use the same command that you would use to rename a file. In DOS systems, to change the name of the directory *save* to *backup*, you would use the command

move save backup

but in UNIX systems, you would use the command

mv dir1 mydir

to change the name of the directory. This operation maintains the same subdirectory hierarchy in the new directory that the old directory had. Also in UNIX systems, you can do the following command

mv newfile1 mydir

which will move the file *newfile1* out of the current directory and into the subdirectory *mydir*. This operation is available on DOS systems using the command **move**. You can use a pattern as the name of the files to move to the directory *mydir* and every file that matches the pattern will be moved to the directory. For example, the command

mv *.dat mydir

will move all files that end in *.dat* to the *mydir* directory.

DELETING FILES AND DIRECTORIES

To delete a file in DOS, you use the **erase** command, while in UNIX you delete a file with the **rm** command. Thus, in DOS systems, the following command will delete a file called *badstuff*:

erase badstuff

while in UNIX systems, the command

rm badstuff

would delete the file *badstuff*. UNIX does not have an **undelete** command as in some DOS systems. On a UNIX system, once you delete a file, it cannot be recovered. In both DOS and UNIX systems, you can use wildcard characters to select a set of files to delete: To delete all the files with names ending in ".o", in DOS systems, you would use the command

erase *.o

while in UNIX you would use the command

rm *.o

which will delete those files whose names end in ".o". If you wanted to delete everything in a directory, in DOS you would issue the command

erase *.*

but on a UNIX system the comparable delete command

rm *.*

would only delete files with names that have a period in them. Thus, the usual command to delete all files in a directory on a UNIX system would be

rm *

which will delete all files except those that begin with a period.

As an additional feature some versions of UNIX allow you to execute the **rm** command in an interactive mode. DOS does not have this. The **rm** command will ask your permission to delete any file that the **rm** command finds. For example, if you execute the following command in the directory */usr/marty*

> **rm -i ***

you will be prompted before each file is deleted with the message

> `delete .cshrc?`

to which you reply "y" or "n" to delete it or not. You will then be asked about the next file in the directory. You can choose to delete any or all of the files that match the specified pattern. If you need to delete a file that has unusual characters in its name such as dollar sign ($) or even number sign (#), you can use the **rm -i *** command to request that everything in the directory be deleted and then only choose to delete the files with the unusual names.

To delete the *baddir* directory, on DOS you would use the command

> **rd baddir**

while on UNIX systems, you would use the command:

> **rmdir baddir**

but as in DOS you cannot delete a directory that is not empty. You must empty the directory first before you can delete it. A common mistake is to attempt to delete a directory and have that operation fail. On DOS **dir** will list all files in a directory. But on UNIX when you use the **ls** command to check the contents of the directory, **ls** will indicate that it is empty. Remember that if you do not add the "-a" option the files that begin with a period will not show up when you use the **ls** command.

UNIX provides several options for the **rm** command to remove the contents of a directory as well as the directory itself. On DOS systems, you would use the command **deltree** as in

> **deltree baddir**

On UNIX systems, for example, if you wanted to remove the directory *baddir* and all its contents, you would issue the command

> **rm -rf baddir**

which will delete the directory *baddir* even if files or even subdirectories still exist in it.

CREATING AND USING ALIAS NAMES
FOR FILES AND DIRECTORIES

Sometimes it is important to refer to a file or a directory by a second name. This might be done to save a user from learning the new name of a file or a directory. It can also be done to pass some information to a program, as we will see. Creating a second name for a file or a device is done with the **ln** command, sometimes called the link command because you are linking two files together. Both files and directories can have aliases.

With a linked file, only one version of the file needs to exist and be maintained, even if the file is known by more than one name. Files in other directories can be accessed from your working directory. A file can have multiple links with different filenames. Links can be broken with the **rm** command but the file still exists. The file can only be removed when *all* physical links are removed. Thus, the command

ln savefile linkedsavefile

will create a second name, *linkedsavefile* for the file *savefile*. The original file must exist before an alias for it can be created. You can determine that a file is a linked file by examining its type with the **ls** command. First, display the characteristics of the *savefile* file with the command

ls -l savefile

and you will see

```
-rw-rw-rw- 1 martya techsupp 463 Jun 14 1993 savefile
```

If you now execute the **ln** command and then executed the command

ls -l savefile linkedsavefile

you would see:

```
-rw-rw-rw- 2 martya techsupp  463 Jun 14 1993 linkedsavefile
-rw-rw-rw- 2 martya techsupp  463 Jun 14 1993 savefile
```

You can determine that *savefile* is linked to another by examining the number just to the right of the access permissions fields all the way on the left. You will notice that the number has increased from 1 to 2. Unfortunately, you cannot easily determine which file is linked to the other except that modifying one will cause the modification date of the other to change.

A second type of alias, a pointer to the file of interest, can also be created. Unfortunately, this type of alias is not always available on every UNIX system. The "symbolic" link command if, available, is easier to use because you can determine which two files are linked. For example, the command

ln -s savefile symlinksavefile

will link the two files together, and you can use the command

ls -l savefile symlinksavefile

to observe the connection between the files. The output will be

```
-rw-rw-rw- 2 martya techsupp  463 Jun 14 1993  savefile
lrwxrwxrwx 1 martya techsupp    8 Dec 21 13:51
                               symlinksavefile@ -> savefile
```

Notice that *symlinksavefile* has a file type of l and that it points to the file that it is linked with.

SEARCHING FOR A FILE

You can search through directories and subdirectories for one file or a set of files by using the **find** command. In its simplest form, the **find** command will display the full pathname of every file that it finds, each name on a separate line.

The first parameter that you specify for the **find** command is which directory to start searching for a named file. The **find** command will examine all subdirectories that it encounters. Thus, the command

find / -print

will generate a list of every file on the system by starting at the root directory and displaying the name of every file the command encounters, as in the following list:

```
/
/tmp
```

```
/tmp/lost+found
/tmp/letter
/tmp/rrnact.19631
/tmp/core
/tmp/active.19391
/usr
/usr/lpp
/usr/lpp/bos
/usr/lpp/bos/inst_root
/usr/lpp/bos/inst_root/etc
/usr/lpp/bos/inst_root/etc/filesystems
/usr/lpp/bos/samples/vca/include
/usr/lpp/bos/samples/vca/include/vcawrap.h
/usr/lpp/bos/samples/vca/lib/mylibXm.h
```

This list of files would be quite lengthy, but it could then be searched for a particular file in which you are interested. For example, if you are looking for the source of a program called *checkit*, you would be interested in any filename that contains the letters *checkit*. If all of the source for a set of programs is kept in the *source/rcs* directory, the following command would find those files

find /source/rcs -print | grep checkit

and a list of files in the directory *source/rcs* that contain the string *checkit* would be displayed. More details on the use of the **grep** command are found in chapter 5. In this use of the **grep** command, any line containing *checkit* will be displayed and all other lines will be deleted.

Often you execute the **find** command with at least one method of qualifying what files you have found. Once a file is found that matches the specified pattern, you can operate on it with a command or just print its fully qualified name. As another example, suppose you are looking for one particular file but you do not know what directory it is in. For example, the command

find / -name passwd -print

will search every directory and subdirectory starting at the root directory for a file named *passwd* and would display the full pathname of any files found.

Several other qualifications are possible. One very useful file qualification parameter is to specify how "new" the file must be. Thus, the command

find / -newer s.b.c -print

would display the names of all files that have been modified more recently than the file *s.b.c.* One fact to remember is that in this context directories are files, too, and any directories that had been modified would be displayed as fitting the qualification. The *type* parameter can be used to select the kind of files in which you are interested. For example, you could create a list of all the directories on your system with the command

find / -type d -print

You can add other criteria to further limit the list of files. Thus, you can exclude directories from your list with another parameter as in the following

find / -newer s.b.c -type f -print

which would display only files (and not directories) that fit the *newer than s.b.c* criteria. Usually this type of command is used to generate a list of files that need to be backed up on tape. One other parameter for creating a backup of recently modified files can be written

find / -newer s.b.c -type f -cpio /dev/rfd0

which would find all of the files that have been modified more recently than *s.b.c* and copy them in *cpio* format to the device */dev/rfd0.*

The **find** command will also execute a command using every file that matches the criteria you have specified as an argument. For example, the command

find /usr/marty -type f -exec ls -l {} \;

will produce a list of all the files in the */usr/marty* directory in the "long" format of the **ls** command, as in

```
-r--r--r--  1 marty  sys  6218 Dec 21 11:42 .cshrc
-rw-------  1 marty  sys   927 Dec 21 12:24 .login
-rw-------  1 marty  sys   811 Dec 21 13:55 .profile
-rw-r-----  1 marty  sys  3185 Oct 21 12:48 letter
```

```
-rw-------   1 marty   sys    281 Dec 21 13:55 mbox
-rw-r--r--   1 marty   sys    795 Oct 25 11:16 memo1
-rw-r--r--   1 marty   sys    456 Oct 25 11:16 oldmemo
```

The left and right curly brackets ({}) represent the names of files that fit the criteria you have specified. The back slash (\) is needed to stop the shell programs from interpreting the special character semicolon (;) before the **find** command can use it.

NAMING UNIX FILES—WHAT ARE VALID UNIX FILENAMES?

In UNIX as in DOS, filenames can contain letters, numbers, and some special characters such as period and underscore. In addition (and this is an important fact!), file and command names on UNIX systems are *case sensitive*. For DOS users this means that you must be aware of whether the CAPS LOCK key is on, because the file named *AAA* is different from the file named *aaa*, and the file named *Aaa* from the file name *aaa*. In DOS systems, you do not need to be aware of your CAPS LOCK key because file names and command names are case insensitive—whether you use capital letters or lowercase letters, the file and command name that you specify will be recognized.

DOS has a set of rules governing how files are named and requiring that for files to perform certain functions they must be named in a certain way. For example, in DOS the names of executables have "EXE" or "COM" to the right of the period. In fact, the period in the name has a special meaning in DOS. The portion of the filename to the right of the period is called the *extension* in DOS and can only be three characters long. In addition, the extension designates that the file has a special function. For example, a file that has an extension of *EXE* or *COM* is an executable.

In UNIX there are almost no naming conventions. Executables can be called anything. In UNIX the period is just another character in the name of a file or executable and has no special significance. In UNIX there can be as many letters to the right of the period as the maximum length of filenames allows. Further, the period can be used more than once in a filename and can even be used to start a filename. Thus, the following are valid filenames:

```
a.b
a.bcdef
.ab
.a.b.c
```

These last two files, starting with period or dot, are sometimes referred to as "hidden files" because the **ls** command does not show their presence when issued with no options.

An important point to understand is that for DOS users, the command

ls *.*

will display all files in a directory, but for UNIX users this command will only display files that have a period in their names. Files whose names are *abc*, *sjsjsjs*, and so on will not be displayed. If you are copying files and use the command

cp *.* newdirectory

on a UNIX system, you will be disappointed with the contents of the directory *newdirectory*, because it will not contain files that do not have a period in their names.

Several other special characters can be used to create lists of objects. Question marks (?) are used to wildcard single characters. For example, examining the file system structure in Figure 3.1, the command

ls -l /usr/marty/docs/ord.?

will display the attributes for the files *ord.2* and *ord.4* but not *ord.12*. Thus, only files that start with *ord.* and have *just* one character to the right of the period will be shown. Another selection method uses the curly brackets:

ls -l ord.{1,2,3}

which would display the attributes of files *ord.2* but not *ord.12* or even *ord.4*. These selection methods can be useful when selecting just certain files on which to operate.

DOS systems limit the format and length of filenames—there can be up to eight characters to the left of the period, and up to three characters to the right of the period. As discussed earlier, the period has no special significance in UNIX systems and is just part of the name. The minimum length of a filename that a UNIX system must allow is 14 characters and includes any periods that are in the filename. Some UNIX systems allow up to 128 characters in a filename, but this is not standard.

One final cautionary note on filenames on UNIX systems: If you try to create a filename with some special character in it, such as "$," "%," or even "&," UNIX *will* allow you to do so. Unfortunately, each of these characters has special meaning for the shell programs under which you are executing, and you will have trouble being able to refer to these files with standard filename notation as discussed earlier in this chapter. Thus, you should avoid using any of these characters in your filenames. If you inadvertently create a file with a name that contains some special character and you wish to delete that file, you can use the **rm -i** command described earlier to delete it.

CONTROLLING FILE ACCESS

In UNIX systems, unlike DOS systems, access to files and directories can be controlled. In chapter 3, in the discussion of the output from the **ls** command, file access permissions were displayed for different files. For example, the command

    ls -l memo1

displayed

```
-rw-r----- 1 marty   techsupp 18417 Jun 18 15:00   memo1
```

The set of ten characters at the left of the line of output indicates first the type of file, and then the access rights for the file. Each file (and directory) has three sets of access privileges, one set for the owner of the file, one set for the group owner of the file, and one set for those users who are not the owner or a member of the group that owns the file. Each set of privileges covers the right to read the file, write the file, or execute the file as shown in Figure 4.1.

If an access right for a particular category of user has been granted, the appropriate letter will appear. If that access right has not been granted, a - (dash) will appear.

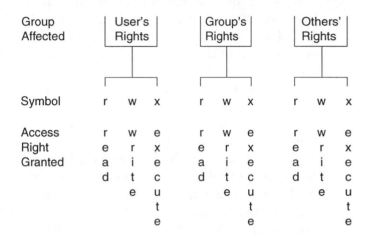

Group Affected	User's Rights			Group's Rights			Others' Rights		
Symbol	r	w	x	r	w	x	r	w	x
Access Right Granted	r e a d	w r i t e	e x e c u t e	r e a d	w r i t e	e x e c u t e	r e a d	w r i t e	e x e c u t e

Figure 4.1.   Access permissions for a file.

Each of these sets of privileges can be controlled independently as decided by the owner of the file (or the root user). Thus, the person who creates a file can decide who can read that file, write into that file, or execute that file. You can observe what permissions have been set for a file by using the **ls** command as discussed in the previous chapter. Thus, the command

ls -l /usr/marty/letter

would show the permissions that the file */usr/marty/letter* has as in

```
-rw-r-----  1 martya techsupp 5185 Oct 21 12:48 letter
```

which would indicate that the owner can read and write this file, members of the *techsupp* group can read this file, and everyone else has no access to this file. Each of these permissions can be managed independently using the **chmod** command. Only the owner or the superuser can modify the access permissions of a file.

The **chmod** command takes either a symbolic or numeric argument to specify what access rights to modify and the name(s) of the files or directories whose rights are being modified. The symbolic argument consists of three fields: (1) which set of users are affected, (2) whether to add or delete the access rights specified by the third field, and (3) which access rights to add or delete. For example, if you, as the owner of the file, wanted to allow everyone to be able to read the file, you would issue a command like

> **chmod a+r /usr/marty/letter**

which would add the permission to read the file for the "a" categories of users (that is, all types of users). Thus, the symbolic argument is three letters with the first indicating which user group, the second indicating what action to take, and third indicating what access right to operate on. More of the various options of the **chmod** command are summarized in Figure 4.2. As another example, you could add the write permission for just the group of users who belong to the *techsupp* group with the command

> **chmod g+w /usr/marty/letter**

and the command

> **ls -l /usr/marty/letter**

would show the permissions of the file */usr/marty/letter*

User Groups:

- u Owner of files
- g Collection of users combined into a special set of users
- o All users who can gain access to system and are not the owner or a member of the group
- a All users regardless of owner or group

Action to Take:

- + Add the access right
- - Subtract the access right

Access Right Types:

- r File can be read
- w File can be written to, deleted, created anew
- x Change directories, copy files, use files as executables

Figure 4.2. Symbolic options for the **chmod** command.

```
-rw-rw-r-- 1 martya techsupp 5185 Oct 21 12:48 letter
```

which would indicate that all users can read this file but only the owner and the users that belong to the *techsupp* group can change it.

The **chmod** command can also take a numeric argument as illustrated in Figure 4.3. To use a numeric argument, you would add the values for the access rights that you wish to grant. As an example of this **chmod** format, consider the command

chmod 666 /usr/marty/letter

What would the command

ls -l /usr/marty/letter

show? The output would be

```
-rw-rw-rw- 1 martya techsupp 5185 Oct 21 12:48 letter
```

which would indicate that all users can both read and write this file.

Access to directories can also be controlled in the same way, except that write access to a directory indicates the right to create a file in the directory. The execute attributes for directories control access to the directory itself. If the execute attribute is not specified, the contents of the directory cannot be searched, nor can a file be written to that directory.

Any combination of values for attributes will work, although

Users Affected Access Right	u	g	o
r (read)	400	40	4
w (write)	200	20	2
x (execute)	100	10	1

Figure 4.3.   Numeric options for the **chmod** command.

some of the combinations may not make very much sense. For example, the command

chmod 234 filename

will change the attributes of *filename* to be

```
--w--wxr--
```

which will allow owner and group members to write over the file, but only the nonowner, nongroup member can read the file. Further, if it is an executable file, only members of the group owner will be able to execute this file.

When you own a file, you can change the owner of that file. To do that, you use the **chown** command. For example, to change the owner of the *badfile* file to root, you would execute the command

chown root badfile

which would change the owner of the file to root. Once you have done that, you cannot change your mind and change it back again. Only the owner, or, of course, root can change the owner of a file. You can also change the group owner of a file that you own using the **chgrp** command. For example, to change the group from *techsupp* to *goodguys* of file *notsobadfile*, you would execute the following command

chgrp goodguys notsobadfile

Of course, you must be the owner of the file to start with.

The permissions that a file has when it is created are set by the current value of the *umask* field ("user mask"). The value of this field only affects new files and has no effect on currently existing files. You can determine the current setting of *umask* by entering the command **umask** by itself with no arguments. The value that is displayed indicates what file access will be *denied* for the various groups of users previously discussed. For example, if the command

umask

displays the value

newly created files will not be writable by members of the group and will not be accessible at all by users who are not the owner or members of the group that owns the file.

A user controls what access to grant others for new files by modifying the value of **umask**. Executing **umask** command with the value you want as the command line argument will set it to that value. For example, if you wish to allow all users the right to read the file but only you will have the right to write into the file, you would set the **umask** value to be "22" with the command

umask 22

Now when you create a file it will have as file access permissions

```
rw-r--r--
```

which gives all users the right to read the file but only the owner can write into the file.

EXAMINING FILES

DOS has strict naming conventions, and thus you can determine what file is an executable by its name. UNIX has no naming convention that would indicate the type of file, and thus, you need a command that will help you to figure out what kind of file you are looking at. The **file** command will analyze the contents of a file and determine what it is (executable, ASCII text, object module, etc.). For example, the command

file .cshrc

will return the message

```
.cshrc: commands text
```

which is true because the *.cshrc* file is used to initialize the environment of a user who is running the **csh** as a shell program. As another example, the command

file /bin/ksh

will display the message

```
/bin/ksh:   executable (RISC System/6000 V3.1)
                  or object module
```

which we would again expect because **/bin/ksh** is an executable. If the examined file contains text, the **file** command will attempt to determine if it is some kind of programming code or if it is just ASCII data. The command

file intro.c

would produce the output

```
intro.c: c program text
```

which is useful information indicating that this is really a file containing C language code. Finally, the output from a command is generally just ASCII data so the command

file ls.out

would generate the output

```
ls.out:  ascii text
```

which we would expect for an ASCII file.

If a file is an ASCII file or one that contains script commands, you can examine it by displaying its contents. An executable can also be examined by using a command that will display any ASCII strings that are found in that executable. The **strings** command will display any sequence of at least four recognizable ASCII characters found in a file, even a file that contains a compiled program. This command can be used if you are receiving an error message and you are not sure what program is generating it. For example, the command

strings passwd

will generate a number of lines of output, one of which contains

```
Must contain at least two alphabetic characters
  and at least one numeric or special character.
```

which indicates one reason why the password that you chose was not accepted. As another example, the message

```
permission denied
```

is actually generated by the shell program. You can determine that by examining the output generated by the **strings** program analysis of the shell program executable. Try the following command

strings /bin/ksh | grep permission

and you will receive the message

```
permission denied
```

indicating that message is generated by the shell program itself.

Exercises

To work on your skill in creating files and directories, you should do the following:

1. Create a file named *inv* using **cat** command and put some ASCII characters into that file. Save the file. How did you do that?
2. Create the following directories: *INV*, *ORD*, *AP*, *AR*, *GL*, *INV1*. What command did you do? Could you create a file named *inv* and a directory named *INV* in DOS system?
3. Verify that the directories are there; is the file *inv* still there? How can you tell the difference between a file and a directory?
4. Attempt to create a file named *INV*. Were you successful? Why or why not?
5. Remove the *INV1* directory and verify that you were successful. How did you make sure that you were successful? Recreate the *INV1* directory.
6. Make *INV* your working directory and verify that *INV* is your working directory. Create a directory in the *INV* directory called *INV1*. Doesn't the *INV1* directory already exist?

7. Now return to your home directory. Use **ls** command with options to get a full listing of the files in your home directory.
8. Examine the contents of the *inv* file. How did you do that? Copy the *inv* file to the *INV* directory. How did you do that? Verify that *inv* is also in the *INV* directory. Verify that the contents of the *inv* files in the two different directories are the same.
9. Move the *inv* file in your home directory to the *INV1* directory. What command did you do to accomplish that? Verify that *inv* is in both the *INV* and the *INV1* directory.
10. Make *INV1* your working directory. Copy the *inv* file to *inv1*. Compare the attributes of *inv* and *inv1*. Are they the same? Remove the *inv* file. How is this different from using the **mv** command to do the same operation?
11. Use **ls** to list all files in your directory that begin with "i". What command did you use? Use **ls** to list all files in your directory that have two character names. What command did you use?
12. Change the access permission on all your files in your home directory to *rwx------*. How did you do that? Will anyone else be able to read or write your files?
13. Create a directory called *testdir*. What attributes does it have? Why? What do they mean? Copy a file into it. What command did you use to do that with? What would have happened if I had misspelled the name of the directory when I executed the previous command?
14. Create a file called *extra*. Change the ownership of *extra* to root. Now change the ownership back.
15. Create a subdirectory *temp*. Now create another name for that subdirectory such as *tmp*. What command did you use? Now display both of these objects. What command did you use? How can you tell that these objects are linked?
16. Executables are compiled to execute on one particular kind of processor. How can you determine which one that is? How can you determine what a file is used for? If a file has the executable attribute turned on, is that an executable?

Text File Operations

OVERVIEW

Text files occupy a special place in both the DOS and UNIX worlds. In DOS systems, system startup files such as *autoexec.bat* and *config.sys* and various *.ini* files provide configuration information in text file format. In UNIX systems, scripts start up the various parts of the UNIX system; these scripts are text files. Certain commands have been created that only work with text files. Commands can display the entire file or just display the beginning of a file or the end of a file. Commands will search text files for strings of text characters. Commands will print text files, too. You can even create text files from the keyboard. The **vi** command, which is used to edit text files, is described in chapter 6.

DISPLAYING TEXT FILES

Displaying a text file on a terminal is done with the **type** command on DOS systems. On UNIX systems you would use the **cat** command. Thus, the command on DOS systems

    type memo1

and the command on UNIX systems

```
cat memo1
```

would cause the complete *memo1* file to be displayed on your terminal from start to finish without pausing. If the file is short, only a few lines or so, or you are only checking to make sure that you have the right file, this command will do what you want. If the file is longer than a few lines and you want to examine that file one group of lines at a time, you will want to use the **more** command.

Displaying a long text file one page of text at a time on a terminal is accomplished with the same command in both DOS and UNIX—the **more** command—but with slightly different syntax. In DOS you would use the command

```
more < memo1
```

while in UNIX the command would be

```
more memo1
```

but the outcome would be the same: The contents of the file *memo1* would be displayed on the terminal one screenful at a time. Thus, the command

```
more manual1.doc
```

would display the first screenful of the contents of the file *manual* and then would stop and display the message

```
--More--
```

At this point you have several options. If you press the **Enter** key, you will see the next line in the file at the bottom of the screen. If you press the space bar at the bottom of the keyboard, you will see a new screenful of text from the file. If you enter the character **q**, the command will quit and return you to the command line. You can page forward with the character **d** or page backward with the character **b**. In addition, you can request some help with **more**'s subcommands by entering the character **h**. Figure 5.1 lists a number of the possible commands that **more** recognizes.

You can also search through the file using the option **/pattern** where you can specify which string you are looking for. If,

```
<space>                    Display next k lines of text
z                          Display next k lines of text
<return>                   Display next k lines of text
d or ctrl-D                Scroll k lines
q or Q or <interrupt>      Exit from more
s                          Skip forward k lines of text
f                          Skip forward k screenfuls of text
b or ctrl-B                Skip backwards k screenfuls of text
'                          Go to place where previous search started
=                          Display current line number
/<regular expression>      Search for kth occurrence of regular expression
n                          Search for kth occurrence of last regular
                             expression
!<cmd> or :!<cmd>          Execute cmd in a subshell
v                          Start up /usr/bin/vi at current line
ctrl-L                     Redraw screen
:n                         Go to kth next file
:p                         Go to kth previous file
:f                         Display current filename and line number
.                          Repeat previous command
```

Figure 5.1. Help screen displayed by **more** command.

for example, you have started examining the file *manual1.doc* as above and at the first prompt, you enter

/fishing

the **more** command will search for the string *fishing* and display a new screen of information with the line that contains the matched pattern shown in the middle of the screen. You can also supply the search pattern when you start up the **more** command as in

more +/fishing manual1.doc

which would cause the **more** command to search through the *manual1.doc* file for the first occurrence of the string *fishing* and to display the page of text on which that string was.

Another useful option for the **more** command is if you enter **v** at the **More** prompt while paging through a file, the file editor **vi** will be started and the line that you are currently on will be the line at which you can start editing the file. This option allows you to look through the file until you find the section that you wish to change and then to edit it.

Two commands enable you to examine just the beginning of a file or just the end of a file without requiring you to look at any part of the file in between. The **head** command will allow you to look at just the first part of a file as in the command

> **head memo1**

which will display the first ten lines of the *memo1* file and then display a command line prompt. Conversely, the command

> **tail memo1**

will display the last ten lines in the *memo1* file before returning and displaying the command line prompt. For each command, you can specify the number of lines that you would like to see, as in the command

> **tail -20 memo1**

which would display the last 20 lines in the *memo1* file. The same option exists for the **head** command. Thus, the command

> **head -20 memo1**

would display the first 20 lines in the *memo1* file.

One additional operation that the **tail** command can do is to display the last lines of a file as it is being created. For example, if you are running a program in another session that writes its output to a file as it generates its reports and you wish to follow the progress that the program is making, you can use the command

> **tail -f logfile**

to display each line of the *logfile* file as the program writes that line to the file. When **tail** command is executed in this fashion, it will continue to run and display lines from the *logfile* until you enter the Ctrl+d key sequence, which will halt the command.

A QUICK WAY TO CREATE A TEXT FILE

In DOS you can create a file from the keyboard with the **copy** command, as in

copy con: letter1

which will create *letter1* with input from the keyboard.

In UNIX you can create a file from the keyboard using the **cat** command, as in

cat > letter1

which takes advantage of the greater than (>) operator, which will redirect all input from the keyboard into the *letter1* file. Redirection is covered in more detail in chapter 7. The cursor would be placed in the first column of your terminal but no prompt would appear. Everything that you type will be stored in file *letter1* until you enter the Ctrl + D key sequence as the first characters on a line. Then the **cat** command will stop and the *letter1* will have been created with the input you entered from the keyboard.

The **cat** command is most useful for creating short text files that are only a few lines long. You can only edit the line that you are currently typing. Any lines already stored in the file cannot be edited with **cat**. Chapter 6 will discuss a text file editor.

Another function that the **cat** command performs is to merge several files together. On DOS systems, the **copy** command will merge files. For example, on a DOS system the command

copy file1+file2+file3+file4 merged_file

would create the *merged_file* file, which would contain the contents of *file1*, *file2*, and so on. On a UNIX system the command to accomplish the same operation would be

cat file1 file2 file3 file4 > merged_file

which would create the *merged_file* file that contains the contents of *file1*, *file2*, and so on. This method of merging files can be performed on any set of files, not just text files.

SEARCHING TEXT FILES FOR A PARTICULAR STRING

In DOS the **find** command searches a file for a string. On UNIX systems the **find** command has a totally different purpose. In UNIX systems the string search operation is done by the **grep** command. Thus, to find the occurrences of a particular string in any text file on a DOS system, you would use the command

find string_to_find file1

while on a UNIX system you would use the command

grep string_to_find file1

which will examine the *file1* file for the existence of the string *string_to_find* and will display each of the lines in which that string is found. In addition, when you use wildcards to search a set of files, the **grep** command will indicate which file contained the particular line that had a match for the search string. Thus, the command

grep subroutine1 *.c

will examine all of the files in the directory that end in *.c* for the existence of the string *subroutine1*.

As in using the DOS **find** command, command line options can be used to modify the behavior of the **grep** command. For example, to display only a count of the matching lines, use the **-c** option; to display the number of the line on which the match occurs use the **-n** option.

To reverse the operation of **grep** and display only those lines in the file that do *not* contain the string, use the **-v** command line option. Thus, if you are searching script files for the use of a particular command or environment variable, and you would not want to see any references that are in lines that are just comments in the scripts, you would use the command sequence

grep TERM script1 | grep -v "\#"

which will search the file *script1* for references to the string *TERM* and will not display any of those matches that begin with the number sign (#) which are comments in script files. This command sequence uses the pipe (|) operator, which will be more fully discussed in chapter 7.

By default the **grep** command is case sensitive and looks for an exact match to the specified pattern following the case of the letters specified. Thus, the command

grep abc file1

will find different matches than the command

> **grep ABC file1**

If you want to find any lines that contain the letters of interest without regard to the case of the letters, you should use the **-i** command line option. Thus, the command

> **grep -i abc file1**

will find the same matched lines as the command

> **grep -i ABC file1**

will find.

COMPARING TEXT FILES

Sometimes you want to check to see if two text files are the same. On DOS systems, the **comp** command will compare two files with any contents and display their differences. On UNIX systems the **diff** command is used to compare two files and can display their differences in an output form that indicates what lines to edit. In its simplest format, the command

> **diff manual1.doc manual1.bak**

will cause the differences between the two files to be displayed, line by line. For each difference between the two files, the lines from each of the two files are displayed one after the other as in

```
2c2
< Snow While and the Seven Dwarfs
---
> Snow White and the Seven Dwarfs
```

which indicates that the second line in the files differ. Further, the **diff** command indicates by the less than (<) operator that *file1* contained the line *Snow While and the Seven Dwarfs* while *file2* contained the line *Snow White and the Seven Dwarfs*.

If files differ because lines have been added to one file or the other, the **diff** command indicates where these new lines were added. The **diff** command attempts to find common lines in the two files to minimize the number of differences between them.

The **diff** command is usually used to compare two ASCII text files but can be used to compare executables.

PRINTING TEXT FILES

In DOS systems the (one and often only) printer is generally attached directly to the computer. In UNIX systems, often there may be several printers, each of which may have a different function or may be located in different places in the building. In the DOS system, you use the **print** command to print a file, while in UNIX systems you use the **lp** command to print a file.

Often you create text files so that you can print them on paper. Printing files is managed by the **lp** command. Much like a DOS environment, the UNIX system contains a print spooler that will receive requests to print a file and will queue up these requests until the printer of interest is ready and available. The **lp** command has a range of commands to assist in informing the print spooler what kind of printer to choose, even what kind of paper, or some other characteristics of how to print the file.

Generally each user has a designated printer. Often this printer is known by its location; if printer pools are being used, the printer will be known by its class. Once a user has an assigned printer, that user will want to print files on that printer. You would do this by directing the **lp** command to print the file on a particular printer using the **-d** option. For example, suppose that a user has *printer1* as the assigned printer, the command

lp -d printer1 file_to_print

will request that the print spooler print the *file_to_print* file on the printer named *printer1*. If this print request is accepted, a message from the print spooler such as

```
request id is printer1-304 (1 file)
```

will be displayed on the terminal, indicating that this printer request was accepted and was assigned the name *printer1-304*. The name assigned to your print request by the print spooler can be used to determine the status of your print request or to cancel the print request using the **cancel** command. To check on the progress of your print request, you can use the **lpstat** command as in

lpstat

which might produce the following output

```
printer1-304  marty  22179  Jan 4 13:59 on printer1
```

which indicates that the print request just made is being printed on *printer1*.

A print request can be canceled by the **cancel** command using the name assigned to the print request, as in

cancel printer1-304

which indicates that the print request *printer1-304* is no longer needed and should be discarded. If this **cancel** command is accepted, the message

```
request "printer1-304" canceled
```

will be displayed.

Sometimes the output that is to be printed needs to be printed later when other reports are ready to print or when the printer is loaded with special forms. The **lp** command can be used to indicate that a print request is queued for later as in

lp -d printer1 -H hold file_to_print_later

which will submit the print request to the print spooler but request that it not be printed at the current time.

After the file has been sent to be printed, the **lpstat** command would show

```
printer1-306  marty  22179  Jan 4 14:00 being held
```

The names of the defined printers and the current contents of the printers' queues are displayed using the **lpstat** command. The command

lpstat -t

will produce a complete listing of all defined printers and other information about the printer spooler as in the following

```
scheduler is running
system default destination: printer1
members of class classa:
    printer1
device for printer1: /dev/lp
classa not accepting requests since Wed Sep 29
    11:47:14 1993 - new destination
printer1 accepting requests since Wed Sep 29 11:50:07
1993
printer printer1 now printing printer1-304. enabled
    since Wed Oct 20 10:45:37 1993. available.
printer1-304 marty 22179 Jan 4 13:59 on printer1
```

which indicates that the print request just made is being printed on *printer1*, that the device is */dev/lp*, and that this printer is the system default printer. If you make a mistake and try to send your print request to a nonexistent printer, the **lp** command will display an error such as

```
lp: ERROR: Destination "printer2" is unknown
to the LP print service.
```

You can specify where print requests will normally be printed by defining the **LPDEST** environment variable. Thus, the following will cause all printed output to be sent to the *dest1* printer to be printed

setenv LPDEST dest1

for the C shell users or

LPDEST=dest1;export LPDEST

for users of Korn shell. Now when you print a file, you will not have to specify the printer destination as in the following command

lp cron.log

which requests the printing of the *cron.log* file and does not specify on which printer to print that file. The output will be sent to *dest1* to be printed because of the value of the *LPDEST* variable.

Exercises

1. Create a text file with a list of animals. Make sure that both "lion" and "tiger" are on your list. What command did you use to do that?
2. Display the file at your terminal. Display only the first line at your terminal. Display only the last line at your terminal.
3. Create a second list of animals. Merge this list with the first list of animals. What command did you use?
4. Search your list of animals for "lion." Did you find a match? Maybe you spelled it "Lion." Search your list of animals again. Display the line number it is on.
5. Print your list of animals. Print only the first two animal names in your list. Print the entries in your file that contain the string "ige."
6. What is your default printer? From the *INV1* directory print the *inv* file on your default printer. Start a print job, use **lpstat** command to find out the status of the job, and then cancel the print job.

Editing Text Files: Using the **vi** Editor

OVERVIEW

Text files are very important in UNIX systems. Historically, UNIX was designed to be an operating system to enable programmers to build systems. Thus, files that contain source code statements were considered very important. Second, script files to simplify tasks that need to be repeated many times are just text files that contain appropriate commands. Both of these kinds of files need to be created and changed. An editor that can accomplish this task with some ease would be a necessary part of any set of tools that an operating system provides.

The **vi** editor is used to edit ASCII files of all sorts on a UNIX system. This editor is geared toward its initial task, which was to edit source files for programmers. It is not a word processor (and is not WYSIWYG, "what you see is what you get") but has the advantage over a word processor in that it does not insert control characters anywhere in the file. The **vi** editor performs the same functions as the **edit** command on DOS systems. In fact, **vi** is the only interactive editor that can always be relied on to be available on a UNIX system.

EDITING OPERATIONS

Starting the vi Editor

To start the **vi** editor, you merely need to specify the **vi** command and the name of the file that you wish to edit. For example, if you want to edit a file named *module1.src*, on DOS systems you would enter the command

edit module1.src

and on UNIX systems you would use the command

vi module1.src

and the **vi** editor would start up by presenting the first 24 lines in the file on the screen and the comment at the bottom

```
"module1.src"  67 lines, 932 words
```

which indicates that the file *module1.src* has 67 lines containing 932 words. If the file did not exist, the message at the bottom of the screen would be:

```
Editing "module1.src (new file)"
```

Thus, you can use **vi** to create a file as well as change an already existing file. The bottom line of the screen will be used for various status messages and various displays of information if you ask for them. No lines of the file will appear there. The rest of the screen is used to display lines in the file. In most cases either 23 or 24 lines of 80 characters each will be displayed.

Unlike the DOS **edit** command, once **vi** is started, the initial state of **vi** is in "command" mode, which means that anything you type will be interpreted as commands that the **vi** command should execute and not as input into the file. You can move around in the file by issuing one of the movement commands shown in Table 6.1. You will notice that there are even commands to move to the left ("h" character) or to the right ("l" character) within a line and to go up ("k" character) or down one line ("j" character). These movement keys are in the middle row on a standard keyboard under the

Table 6.1.   **vi** Commands to Move around in File

Move Operation Desired	vi Command
Move Left One Character	h
Move Up One Line	k
Move Down One Line	j
Move Right One Character	l
Move Right to Beginning of Next Word	w
Move Right to End of Word	e
Move Left to Beginning of Word	b
Move Up One Half Screen	^u
Move Backwards One Screen	^b
Move Down One Half Screen	^d
Move Forward One Screen	^f
Move to End of Current Line	$
Move to Beginning of Line	0
Move to First Line on Screen	H
Move to Last Line on Screen	L
Move to First Nonblank on Next Line	+
Move to First Nonblank on Prev Line	-
Go to line n	nG
Go to end of file	G
Search Forward for the String "xxx"	/xxx
Search Backward for the String "xxx"	?xxx
Repeat Last Search	n

Note: "^" indicates holding down the key labeled "Ctrl" while entering the required character.

right hand. Early UNIX terminals did not have arrow keys, so movement commands needed to be defined. Users are now accustomed to using the arrow keys to move around in a file, so today's implementation of **vi** recognizes the arrow keys as movement keys. By the way, these movement commands do not change anything—they just position the cursor.

Lines of text can be changed by entering one of the commands shown in Table 6.2. These commands change text that *already*

Table 6.2.   **vi** Commands to Manipulate Text

Text Manipulation Operation	vi Command
Delete Character	x
Reverse Two Characters	xp
Delete n Words	ndw
Change n Words	ncw
Replace One Character	r
Replace Characters until Escape Key	R
Delete n Lines	ndd
Undo Last Command	u
Join This Line with Next	J

exists in the file. But you can't insert text in this mode. To do that, you must be in "insert" mode, which is entered by using one of the insert commands listed in Table 6.3. Once in insert mode, you remain in insert mode until you push the **Escape** key, after which you will be returned to the command mode. Thus, **vi** is a bimodal editor—you are always in one of these two states, command mode or insert mode.

Table 6.3.   **vi** Commands to Enter and Leave Insert Mode

Begin / End Insert Operation	vi Command
Begin Insert Mode after Current Character	i
Begin Insert Mode before Current Character	a
Begin Insert Mode at End of Line	A
Begin Insert Mode after Current Line	o
Begin Insert Mode before Current Line	O
Begin Replace Mode at Current Character	R
End Insert Mode	esc key
Yank n lines	ny
Insert Lines after Current Line	p
Insert Lines before Current Line	P

Moving around in a File

Terminals on early UNIX systems had very limited text display characteristics, were quite slow (110 Baud), and had no arrow keys. Thus, developers placed a high premium on being able to move around easily in a file with as few characters as possible. Because of these concerns, **vi** provides a large number of single character commands just designed to move around in a file. In fact, almost every character, lower case and upper case, is a command. To move up a line, use the **k** character, and move down a line with the **l** character. Move to the left one character with the **j** character and to the right with the **k** character. To move to the beginning of the next word in a line, use the **w** character; to the end of the current word, use **e**; to the beginning of the word to the left use the **b** character. Finally, you can move to the end of the current line by using a **$** character and to the beginning of the current line with a **0** (zero) character. On today's modern terminals, arrow keys can also be used to move you around in a file.

You can search through a file for a particular string using the forward slash (/) command to search forward or the question mark (?) to search backward. In both cases you just add the text for which you are looking to the appropriate search command and the string will be found. You can repeat the last search command (in either direction) by using the **n** command.

Deleting and Changing Text in a File

You can delete the one character highlighted by the cursor by entering the command **x**, the one word by entering the command **dw** and the one line by entering the command **dd**. You can delete multiple characters, words, or lines by preceding the appropriate command with the count of characters, words, or lines to delete. For example, the command

> **x**

will delete one character, while the command

> **4x**

will delete the next four characters in the file. The command

dw

will delete one word while the command

6dw

will delete the next six words in the file. The command

3dd

will delete three lines. The **vi** command will even delete across lines when deleting characters or words.

You can replace text one character at a time using the **r** command. Thus, entering the **r** command will make the next character you enter replace just the one your cursor is on. If you want to type over some characters and replace them with an equivalent number of characters, you would use the **R** command. In this case you will continue to replace what is in the file, one character at a time, until you touch the **Escape** key.

Inserting Text in a File

You insert text into a file using **vi** by entering the insert mode with one of the commands in Table 6.3. Once in the insert mode, any character you type (including carriage returns and control characters) will be inserted into the file. You return to the command mode by pushing the **Escape** key (Esc). All of the insert commands operate in the same manner, but where you start the insert process is different. If you want to start inserting at the current cursor position, you would use the command **i**; at the end of the current line, the command **A**; before the current line, the command **O**; and after the current line, the command **o**.

One insert command deserves special mention: The **ncw** command puts you in insert mode after **vi** has deleted the "n" words that you requested. Thus, this command is a combination of delete and insert. In addition, the words to be replaced are still displayed with a dollar sign ($) indicating where they end. You will stay in insert mode until you press the **Escape** key. Thus, you can insert as many words as you wish, even more than were originally present in the file. When you begin entering data, it will write over the data that is currently displayed on your screen.

Cut and paste operations are done by use of the delete commands and the **p** (put) commands. You would delete the characters, words, or lines that you wish to move and then put them in the place in the file where you want them. Thus, the command

3dd

would delete three lines. You would move to the place in the file where you wanted to place those three lines and issue the command

p

if you wanted them to appear before the current line and the command;

P

if you wanted them to appear after the current line.

You can copy a set of lines to another place in the file using the **y** (yank) command to copy the lines into a buffer and the **p** command to place them into the file. Thus, the command

4yy

would copy the next four lines and the command

p

would place them before the current line.

Reading and Writing Files from within vi

As discussed in a previous section, you can save your edited file and exit from **vi** using the **ZZ** command. If you just want to save the file without exiting **vi**, you would use the **:w** command. If you want to exit **vi**, you would use the **:q** command. If you have made changes, you will not be allowed to exit **vi**. If you have made changes to a file but do not want to save those changes, you can use the **:q!** command.

Reading and writing files from within **vi** can be a convenient way to create new files from old files, to combine pieces of files into larger ones, or to break up one file into smaller pieces. The various commands to do these operations are shown in Table 6.4.

Table 6.4.   Basic **vi** File Operations

vi File Operation	*vi* Command
Insert contents of another file	**:r filename**
Insert output from command execution	**:r!command**
Write the updated file	**:w**
Write to a new file	**:w filename**
Write a portion of a file	**:m,nw filename**
Edit a new file	**:e filename**
Quit **vi**	**:q**
Quit **vi** and save the file	**ZZ** or **:x**
Quit **vi** without saving	**:q!**

Each of these file-based commands is part of the set of commands available via the ":" operator.

You can insert the contents of one file before the current line in the file by using the ":r" operator. For example,

:r otherfile

will insert the contents of the *otherfile* file before the current line.

You can also create a new file that contains all or part of the current file. To create a file with all of the current file use the command

:w newfile

which will write the entire current contents of the file into a new file *newfile*. This command will fail if the file already exists. If you wish to overwrite a currently existing file, you need to add an "!" after the "w" command as in

:w! newfile

which will overwrite an already existing file with the contents of the current file. But suppose you only wish to write part of the current file out as a new file. To do that you would add the line numbers that designate the first line through to the last line that you wish to have in the new file. For example, the command

:40,50w afewlines

will write the contents of lines 40 through 50 into a file called *afewlines*. When specifying lines to operate on, you can use dot to mean the current line, and dollar sign to mean the last line of the file. Relative line numbers such as ".+4" or ".-5" can also be used as long as the lines to which you refer do exist in the file. Thus, the above command could be written as

40g (to place you on the right line)
:.,.+10w afewlines

which moves you to the correct position in the file and then writes out the next 11 lines.

You can run a non-**vi** command without leaving **vi** by using the escape to the shell operator ("!") to get to a command prompt. Once at the command prompt you can run any UNIX command without disturbing the file that you are currently editing. If you need to examine another document or calculate some quantity, you can do this outside of **vi** without ending the editing session. In addition, you can use the combination of reading in a file (":r" operation) with the escape to the shell ("!") operation to capture the output of a command into a file. Thus, the operation **:r!command** will capture the output of **command** into a file while editing the file. For example, the command

:r!ls

will read the names of the files in the current directory into the current file.

Cutting and Pasting with vi

The **vi** command offers a set of buffers for storing text. One set of buffers is named for the lowercase letters in the alphabet as in a, b, c, and so on. You put text into such a buffer using the apostrophe (') operator. For example, to put the next five lines in a file into the "g" buffer, use the command

'g5yy

which means yank the next five lines and put them into buffer "g". Now you would move to the place in the file where you wanted to insert those lines. To insert the contents of buffer "g" before the current line, you would use the command

'gp

which will write the current contents of buffer "g" into the file at the current line.

You can perform the cut and paste operations by deleting the lines you move into a buffer and then pasting them into the file at the place you wanted. For example,

'g5dd

will delete the next five lines and store them in buffer "g." To insert the contents of buffer "g" before the current line, you would use the command

'gp

which will write the current contents of buffer "g" into the file at the current line. The contents of a buffer remain the same until another operation is performed that changes its contents.

Deleted items are also saved in buffers. These buffers are numbered from 1 to 10. You retrieve from these numbered buffers in the same way you retrieve from the lettered ones, but you can only put text into these buffers by performing delete operations. Every delete operation causes the deleted text to go into an unnumbered and unlettered buffer. What was previously in the unnumbered buffer is put into buffer 1 and what was previously in buffer 1 is put into buffer 2 and so on. Whatever was in buffer 10 is lost. Thus, the command

'4p

would insert the contents of buffer 4 into the current file before the current line.

The **vi** buffer commands are summarized in Table 6.5.

GLOBAL EDITING AND OTHER ADVANCED vi OPERATIONS

Editing operations that require global changes to a file can be performed from within **vi**. To accomplish a change that affects more than one line you would use the ":s" operator. You can de-

Table 6.5. **vi** Buffer Commands

Buffer Commands	*vi* Command
Put n lines in buffer a	**'anyy**
Put n lines in buffer a and delete from file	**'andd**
Insert lines from buffer a after current line	**'ap**
Insert lines from buffer a before current line	**'aP**

fine which lines in your file will be changed as part of the syntax
tor this command. As an example, to change the first occurrence
of the string "abc" to "def" on every line in the file you would enter
the command

:1,$s/abc/def/

where the range of lines to be changed is entered before the actual **s** command is entered. You can enter the actual line numbers that you wish to change. The dollar sign indicates the last
line in the file. The syntax for the "s" operator requires that some
character—in this example, a forward slash—separates the
string to search for from the one that will replace any string
matches that are found. This version of the command will only
replace the first occurrence in each line. If you wish to replace
every occurrence of the string on a line, you would want to add
the "g" (global) operator at the end of the replacement string.

You can request that only certain lines be eligible for replacement operations. For example, the command

:7,15s/more/less/g

will change every occurrence of "more" to "less" on lines 7 to 15
only. If the range covers lines in the file that do not exist, you will
receive an error message and the operation will not be performed.
If you are not pleased with the substitutions that took place, you
can go back to the "before" version of the file by using the **u** (undo)
command.

If you need to replace a string that contains the slash charac-

Table 6.6. Advanced **vi** Editing Operations

Advanced Editing Operation	vi Command
Change one string to another	**:m,ns/abc/def/**
Display line number	**^g**
Redraw screen	**^l**
Repeat last command	**. (dot)**
Escape to shell	**!**
Insert a control character	**^v**

ter, you can use another character to delimit the search and replace the string. (See Table 6.6.)

PRACTICING vi COMMANDS

The only way to gain ease with the **vi** editor is to use it. You
must practice on various files and become familiar with the
editor's functions. One function that **vi** does not do is to keep a
copy of the file that you are editing. You must do that yourself.
So the first thing to do is to make a copy of any file that you are
worried about editing. You should practice on a simple file that
has just a few lines. For example, create the following file using
the **cat** command:

```
sleepy
happy
sneezy
grumpy
gloomy
```

Make a copy of this file. Now edit this file with **vi** and add the line
Snow White at the end of the file by moving your cursor to the last
line in the file and entering the letter **o**. Now type in the line
Snow White and push the **Escape** key. Use your cursor to move
to the top of the file. Now change the first word to *harry* with the
cw command. Don't forget to press the **Escape** key after you
have typed in your replacement word. Now search for the next

occurrence of *gloomy* using the **/gloomy** command. Change the *o* to an *e* and the next *o* to an *a* using the **r** command. Your file should look like:

```
harry
happy
sneezy
grumpy
gleamy
Snow White
```

Does your file look the same?

Move to the top of the file by using the **lg** command and enter insert mode with the **i** command. Enter the line *Some of the dwards that snow white knew:*. Exit insert mode by touching the **Escape** key. Your cursor will now be at the end of the first line. You can move to the beginning of the word *dwards* by using the **b** command to move to the beginning of the word to the left. Now move to the right using the **l** key until the cursor is under the **d** character in **dward**. Change this character to an **f** by entering the command **rf**. Now your file should look like:

```
Some of the dwarfs that snow white knew:
harry
happy
sneezy
gleamy
grumpy
Snow White
```

But *Snow White* does not belong in the list. Move to that line with the **/Snow** command and then remove that line with the **dd** command. Now your file should look like

```
Some of the dwarfs that snow white knew:
harry
happy
sneezy
gleamy
grumpy
```

You can undo your last change with the **u** command. Try it and see what happens. A second **u** command will redo the operation you requested earlier. Move back up in the file and change *harry* to *sleepy* and *gleamy* to *doc*. Now that the contents of the file are as you want, you can save the file and exit **vi** with the **ZZ** command.

Exercises

To work on your skill in using **vi**, you should do the following exercise. The later steps in this exercise depend on performing the earlier steps.

1. Edit a new file with **vi**. Are you sure that this is a new file? How do you know?
2. Enter the following lines: (For the purposes of this exercise, you should enter the lines exactly as shown, including the carriage returns)

    Now is the time for all good men to come to the adi of thier country.
3. Now change the word "men" to "people." Reverse the last two characters in the word "adi" to "aid." Fix the word "thier." Add the words "who are all available" before "to come to."
4. Add a carriage return after the word "available." Join the next two lines together.
5. Copy the two lines that you have and create two new ones after these two. Save this file as *aid* and exit from **vi**.
6. Now edit a new file called *first*. Add the following lines to this file:

    This is the first line.
    This is the second line.
    This is the third line.
    This is the fourth line.
    This is the fifth line.
    This is the sixth line.

    Is there any easier way to enter this without typing in each line in turn?

7. Read in the *aid* file after the third line. Indent by five spaces each of the lines from the *aid* file that you just read in.

8. Move the last two lines of the inserted file after the line that contains "fourth" and move the first two lines of the inserted file before the line that contains "third." Save this file and print it.

7

Running Applications

OVERVIEW

Running applications means managing input to a set of programs and output from a set of programs. This chapter will examine the various ways both of these sets of operations can be managed. Both UNIX and DOS systems provide functions to send output from a program to a file or to another program. This operation, called redirection, is described first. UNIX offers a facility that DOS does not offer, that of running a program disconnected from a terminal. In UNIX systems, this facility is called running a program in the *background*. This chapter will discuss this background facility. Determining whether a particular background job is still executing can be important to managing applications. The process status command is reviewed so that the status of a program can be determined. How to cancel the execution of a job is also discussed in this chapter. Scheduling a program to execute at a particular time is a function that UNIX systems provide; this facility is explored in this chapter.

REDIRECTING INPUT AND OUTPUT

On both DOS and UNIX, when you execute a command, input is expected from the keyboard of the terminal and output is shown on the terminal's monitor. The input stream is called *Standard Input* and the output stream is called *Standard Output*. There is a third stream of information called *Standard Error*, which, like Standard Output, is an output stream and contains the errors generated by the application. By default, all of these streams of data are expected to be written to or read from the terminal. Instead, you may wish that the output be written to a file or that the input be read from a file. On both DOS and UNIX, performing either of these operations is called *redirection*, because you are changing the direction of the input or output stream. These redirecting operations are accomplished using special operators; Table 7.1 lists the redirection operators and their use.

On both DOS and UNIX, you can send output to a file rather than to the terminal screen using the greater than operator as in

ls -l > ls_long_list

which would place the output of the **ls -l** command into the *ls_long_list* file rather than display it on the terminal. If the *ls_long_list* file already exists, the output from the **ls -l** command will replace whatever its current contents are. The *ls_long_list* file contains every character that would have been written to the terminal. A shell option exists that will prevent the overwriting of the current contents of an already existing file.

The output redirection operator is often used to save the output from the execution of an application program to examine later for problems with the execution. For example, if application program **inv** read in a file of inventory transactions and reported

Table 7.1.   Redirection Operations and Operators

Redirection Operation	*Redirection Operator*
Input read from a file	<
Input read from the terminal until eof is signalled	<<
Output written to a file	>
Output appended to a file	>>
Output written to a program	|

on those transactions, you might want to save that output for some later time. The command

inv > inv.log

will write the output from the **inv** command in the file *inv.log* to be examined at a later date.

Another particularly useful way to use the output redirection operator is to make the output from an application disappear. The way to do that is to redirect that output into the */dev/null* device, the "UNIX system bit bucket." In DOS, you would use the device *NUL:*. Thus, the command

inv > /dev/null

will cause the output to disappear into the bit bucket.

You can append the output from a command into an existing file using the double greater than operator as in

lpstat >> ls_long_list

which will add the output from the **lpstat** command to the current contents of the *ls_long_list* file. Thus, you can build a file that contains the output from several commands. If the file does not exist, it will be newly created.

Usually input into a program comes from the keyboard. But you can accept input from a source other than the keyboard using the less than (<) operator as in

mail harold < letter_to_harold

which will mail the *letter_to_harold* file to the user "harold."

You can combine output redirection with input redirection as in the command

inv > inv.log < inv.trans

which will read the transactions from the *inv.trans* file and will write the output into the *inv.log* file. You can specify these redirection operations in any order.

One special input redirection operator exists that allows input from the keyboard to be passed to a program for a certain period of time. Thus, you can send the input into a program from the keyboard and end the input when you are finished creating the input. This type of redirection is accomplished using the double less than signs (<<) followed by a set of characters to use to signal the end of the input stream. Thus, the command

cat newfile << EOF

will cause all of the input from the keyboard to be copied to the file *newfile* until the characters "EOF" are found at the beginning of a line, which causes the input operation to cease. Any set of characters can signal the end of input and should be chosen not to conflict with the input to the file from the keyboard. This type of redirection is often used to create a file in a shell script because if the names of variables are used in the redirected input stream, they will be replaced by current shell values.

PIPE OPERATIONS

In both UNIX and DOS systems, you can send output from one program directly into another program. On both UNIX and DOS systems, this redirection operation is known as *piping* and uses the pipe operator (|) as in

sort file1 | grep good

which will **sort** the contents of the *file1* file and then keep only the lines that contain the letters "good" and display that output on the terminal.

Pipes are used to connect two commands so that the standard output of one command becomes the standard input to another command. The pipe operator (|) is used to indicate just such a connection. The pipe command format looks like:

commanda | commandb

which would cause the output from the **commanda** command to be sent to **commandb** command as input. More than one pipe operator can be used in a command line. For example, the command

commanda | commandb | commandc

would cause the output from **commanda** to be sent as input to **commandb**, the output from which will be sent as input to **commandc**. The format of the pipe command is the same for both UNIX and DOS systems, but in UNIX systems no temporary files are needed and the pipe operation proceeds from right to left one line at a time. Thus, all pipe-connected commands are executing at the same time. You specify the options for each of the commands just as you would on the command line. Just be sure that the options for each command are given before the pipe command for the next command.

As an example of a pipe operation, suppose you wanted to display a number of lines from the middle of a text file. To do that, you would combine two commands that were described in chapter 5—the **head** command and the **tail** command. Thus, the command

tail -30 memo1 | head -5

will display just the first five lines, starting 30 lines from the end of the file. As another example, suppose you wanted to limit the number of lines that will be displayed as the output of a command. For example, the command

grep "#" script1 | head -5

will display only the first five lines in the *script1* file that are comments.

The output redirection requested by the pipe command will redirect all of the output from a command as input to the next command. Sometimes the output of a command needs to be both displayed and captured into a file. For example, the output from the creation of a multi-diskette **tar** image would be nice to save into a file, but it also would be important to display the message as the **tar** image is built, so that if another floppy diskette is needed, the message will be displayed and can be acted upon. But the command

tar cvmarty > tar.out

will write all of the output from **tar** (except for diagnostic errors) to the file *tar.out*. The **tee** command will display all its input on the terminal and will also copy the input to a file. Thus, the above command would be modified as

tar cvmarty | tee tar.out

and all of the output from the **tar** command will be displayed on the terminal as well as written to the *tar.out* file. As another example, suppose you were counting the files that should be put into the archive with the command

    tar cvmarty | wc -l

But if one of the messages was to insert another diskette, you would not see that message. You can modify the above command so that of the output from **tar** as input to **wc**.

    tar cvmarty | tee tar.out | wc -l

and the output from **tar** would be captured into the *tar.out* file and would also be displayed on the terminal. If the *tar.out* file exists and you want to add to it, you would add an option to the command line as in

    tar cvmarty | tee -a tar.out | wc -l

and the output of **tar** would be added to the *tar.out* file after the current contents of the *tar.out* file.

CREATING AND EXECUTING BATCH FILES

On DOS systems you would create a batch file to execute a set of commands. In the batch file, you could code in looping and conditional tests, and so on. This batch file would have a name that ended in *.bat*. You would create this batch file using any editor that can create text files. On UNIX systems batch files are usually called *scripts*, contain the same kind of commands as you would enter from the command line, and are created using an ASCII editor such as **vi** (which was discussed in chapter 6). The major difference between DOS and UNIX in creating batch files is that in UNIX these batch files can have any name. The idea of a batch file remains the same; they are collections of commands that need to be executed in a particular sequence.

On UNIX systems each of the shell programs provides its own syntax for condition testing, looping, branching, and so on. The script language is much richer in UNIX than in DOS because the idea of doing several operations at the same time is built into the UNIX system but not into DOS. Later chapters will discuss how the script language provided by the shell is used.

RUNNING PROGRAMS AND SCRIPTS IN THE BACKGROUND

On DOS and UNIX when you execute a program from your terminal, no additional commands can be given while the program is executing. If the execution of the program takes a lengthy period of time, you will be unable to use your terminal while this is occurring. On UNIX you can overcome this limitation by running the program in the background, that is to say, not attached to a particular terminal. You accomplish this operation by attaching an ampersand (&) to the end of the command when you enter it on the command line. When the system accepts your command to run in the background, you will receive a notification of the number of the process. As an example, suppose you entered the command

ls -R / > ls-R.out &

you would receive output like

```
[1] 2345
```

indicating that this is the first job currently running in the background during this session and its process number is 2345. You can find out how your command is doing with the command

jobs

which will list all currently executing processes that were started during this session, as in

```
[1] Running  ls -R ...
```

which indicates what state the command is in and even which command you executed.

If you forgot to specify the ampersand (&) at the end of the command that you entered, you can still put the command into the background by using a two-step process. First, you need to interrupt the processing of your command by entering the **Control-Z** character. This operation halts the command but does not end it. The process is suspended. Next, you can put the halted command into the background by using the command

bg %1

which will cause the command to resume processing in the background. You can put as many commands in the background as you wish and you can interrupt the execution of as many commands as you wish.

Commands placed in the background will continue to run as long as they do not generate output to the terminal or require input from the terminal. When either event occurs, the process will suspend operation but will not stop if the user session that began that job is still available. If the user session has ended, the process will be ended.

You can bring that background process into the foreground and satisfy its request for input or output with the command

   fg %1

which will allow that command to display any pending output and for you to give input to that process from your terminal.

You can then put that job back into the background using the **Control-Z** operation to interrupt the foreground job and the command

   bg %1

to start it running in the background once again. Recalling a process from the background and returning it to the background can be repeated as long as you do not log out and end the user session that started the commands. Once the connection to the user session is broken, jobs cannot be retrieved from the background.

When you attempt to log out of a user session and jobs are still pending, you will receive a message, "Jobs still pending," indicating that there are processes in some suspended state. If you still log out after receiving this message, these jobs will be lost.

USING PROCESS MANAGEMENT COMMANDS

On UNIX a report on the processes that you are currently executing would be obtained by using the **ps** command.

   ps

will report process id, the port (tty) that is associated with the process, CPU time it has taken, and the command that was issued for the commands that are currently executing that belong to this session. The following is some sample output from a **ps** command:

```
PID    TTY     TIME    CMD
11444  p0      0:05    csh
11449  p0      0:00    script
11450  p0      0:00    script
11451  p1      0:00    csh
11453  p1      0:00    ps
```

You can get an expanded report that will add the name of the user that started the command, the process id of parent process, the priority of process, and the time the process was started (other information is available, too) using some of the options of the **ps** command. For example,

ps -f

will display all of the processes currently running on the system in the "full" format, which will look something like Figure 7.1. This type of report indicates even which process started each of the processes currently running, that is, the parent process, by adding a column called *PPID*, Parent Process ID. As an example, the process 11444 (*script*) was started by the process 11443 (*csh*).

The **ps** command will report only on processes that you started in this user session. If you want to know all the processes that you have started that are running on the system, you would add the **-u** option with your user name. Thus, the command

ps -u marty

will display the status of any process that the user *marty* started that are still running.

```
UID    PID    PPID   C   STIME     TTY    TIME  CMD
marty  11444  11443  0   10:39:06  p0     0:05  -csh
marty  11449  11444  0   10:39:34  p0     0:00  script
marty  11450  11449  1   10:39:34  p0     0:00  script
marty  11451  11450  3   10:39:34  p1     0:00  sh -i
marty  11454  11451  23  10:39:57  p1     0:00  ps -fu marty
```

Figure 7.1.   Output from a **ps -f** command.

You can also request the status of a process by specifying the number of the process. For example, if you wanted to check on the command started earlier in this chapter with the process id of 2345, you would issue the command

ps -p2345

which would display something like

```
PID   TTY  TIME  COMMAND
2345  p0   0:03  ls -lR
```

If you wanted to make sure it was still processing, you might have to issue this command several times to see if it was still processing.

If you wish to stop a process from running any further you can use the **kill** command with the number of the process. To find out the number of the process, you will have to use one of the process status reports described earlier. For example, suppose that a process you had started was just looping and not accomplishing anything. You could determine its process id with a **ps** command and then use a **kill** command to halt its processing. You must be the owner of the process in order to stop its processing. For example, an example earlier in the chapter started the **ls -lR** command in the background and its process id was 2345. To halt its processing you would use the command

kill 2345

which will stop the processing of job 2345 if the process is interruptible. This form of the **kill** command sends an interrupt signal to the process to indicate that you wish it to stop. Processes can get into a state where they will not respond to that interrupt signal. If this is the case, you will have to use the **-9** option on the **kill** command, which is a system process halt and is effective regardless of the state of the process.

SCHEDULING PROCESSES TO EXECUTE AT A CERTAIN TIME AND DAY

UNIX systems provide a server called **cron** that will execute commands at scheduled times. **cron** is started when the system is initialized, and it runs continuously while the system is running. When **cron** is restarted due to the system restarting, it will reestablish the schedule that it had when the system restart was performed. Each individual user creates its own schedule of commands to execute and then requests the **cron** server to execute them.

The user requests services from the **cron** server using the **crontab** command. The user creates a schedule using a text file editor and then passes that schedule to the **cron** server to be scheduled by executing the **crontab** command with the file as input. Each of these schedule requests have the format

15 02 * * * /usr/marty/pgm1 > /usr/marty/pgm1.out

where the first five entries specify when to execute this entry and the rest of the line is the command to be executed at those times. The five time-to-run fields are, in order from left to right, which minute, which hour, which day, which month, and which day of week, to run the command. One or more spaces separate individual time-to-run fields. An asterisk (*) in the field indicates "every" while a number indicates a particular value. Multiple values can be entered in a field as numbers separated by commas (,). Times are based on 24-hour clocks. For day of week Sunday is 0, Monday is 1, and so on. The example above requests that the command

/usr/marty/pgm1 > /usr/marty/pgm1.out

be executed at 2:15 AM on every day of every month.

Each user can request services from the **cron** server, provided they have been authorized by having their name in the */usr/lib/cron.allow* file. Each user's schedule is managed independently.

When **cron** runs a program for you, it uses the **sh** program and does not establish very much of an environment, other than the *HOME* and *USERNAME* variables. Thus, you must define every other environment variable your program needs (for example, the *TERM* variable or possibly the *LPDEST* variable).

cron will send you mail if your **cron** job fails to execute or if your **cron** job generates any output. But **cron** will *not* remember what parts of the schedule were not run because the system was unavailable.

You use the **crontab -l** command to list your **crontab** entries. The **crontab filename** command will install **crontab** entries.

Your file *filename* contains the **crontab** entries that specify the schedule. Finally the **crontab -r** command will remove your own **crontab** entries. An individual user can only have one schedule of commands to execute. Thus, each time the **crontab filename** command is executed, the schedule for an individual is replaced.

The following is an example of a set of scheduled programs you might choose to run:

```
00  02  * * 1,2,3,4,5,6   /etc/make_incremental_backup
00  02  * * 0             /etc/make_weekly_backup
00  04  01 * *            /etc/make_monthly_backup
```

This schedule might be the master schedule of system backups. In this schedule, an incremental backup is made on Mondays, Tuesdays, and so on, at 2:00 AM. A weekly backup is made on Sunday at 2:00 AM, and a master monthly backup is made on the first day of the month at 4:00 AM.

You can schedule a process (or script) to execute at a particular time and day using the **at** command as in

at 12:15 /usr/marty/pgm1 > /usr/marty/pgm1.out

which would request that this command be run at the next 12:15. The time can include a specification of the date to run the command on.

Exercises

This set of lab exercises will give you practice in using some of the functions described in this chapter.

1. Create a list of all the files that are in your home directory. What command did you use? Can you think of another command to do the same operation?
2. What does the following command and input stream accomplish?

   cat assorted << ZYZYZ
   abcde
   fghij
   klmno

pgrst
uvwxy
z
EOF
ZYZYZ

How many lines in the file *assorted*? What command would you issue to count the lines in that file?

3. Create a letter that you want to send to another user on your system. Use the **mail** command to send that letter.

4. Enter the **ps** command with no arguments. What information is displayed?

5. There are four common arguments used with the **ps** command: *-a*, *-e*, *-l*, and *-f*. Try the command with each option and create a table that lists how the output differs. Which command provides the most information about processes? Which command provides information about the most processes?

6. Find all the processes that you started. Remember that you could have started some processes in a previous session. Use the **ps** command with a pipe and the **grep** command. Use a **kill pid** command to terminate your user process. What happens when you do that?

7. For example, suppose you had a list of animals in the file *animals* and you wanted to produce a list of *animals* in sorted order on your terminal and also into a file. What would the command be?

8. Create the **cron** file to run the job **got_to_make_the_donuts** to run at 4 AM every morning except Sunday. Create a **cron** file to run the job **got_to_make_the_coffee** every two hours Monday through Friday, every one hour on Saturday, and every four hours on Sunday.

Introduction to the UNIX Shells

OVERVIEW

The UNIX shell programs provide a set of functions all on their own just like the **COMMAND.COM** command in DOS. As illustrated in Figure 1.4, the user interacts with UNIX systems through the shell program. For both DOS and UNIX systems, the functionality of these shell programs includes everything from managing the working directory to executing scripts to controlling a variety of operations. For UNIX systems, the shell program provides functions to enable the user to create its own environment. In UNIX systems there are several shell programs available. While each of these shell programs provides some features that the other shell programs do not, many features are common to all of the shell programs. This chapter will discuss some of the facilities that most shell programs provide. Chapters 9 and 10 will discuss the functioning of the Korn and C shell programs in detail.

WHAT UNIX SHELL PROGRAMS EXIST

When you first log in, the prompt you see is usually the default prompt for a particular shell. For example, the Bourne shell usually has a dollar sign ($) as the prompt, the Korn shell has the number sign (#), and the C shell has the dollar sign. Because of this, you can usually guess what shell you are running by examining the prompt. There are other methods that we will discuss later. These prompts can be changed, but it is usually a good idea to only add information to the prompt and leave the character that distinguishes the type of shell.

ENVIRONMENT VARIABLES

Environment variables are used to communicate between the user and various user commands. In DOS systems the **set** command is used to define them. While each of the different shell programs provides its own method to define environment variables, some of the environment variables have the same meaning whether you are using the Korn shell or the C shell.

Each shell program uses a number of environment variables to provide services, such as locating programs to execute, identifying the name of the user's home directory, and so on. These variables are user configurable. You should recognize one particular variable, the *PATH* variable, because it is the same variable that on DOS systems provides a list of directories to search for an executable file. One advantage of UNIX is that an unlimited number of directories can be listed in the *PATH* variable. Another variable, the *PROMPT* variable, which defines what prompt is displayed each time the system asks for a command, is used much the same way on UNIX systems as on DOS systems. Other variables that the shells use have no matches on a DOS system and are discussed in the next two chapters.

Any number of other variables can be defined by a user. Unlike DOS systems, there is virtually no limit to the number of variables that can be defined on a UNIX system. Usually these variables are used by programs to modify their behavior because the value of a variable can be read (or written) by a program (by almost the same system call on both DOS and UNIX systems). The name of a variable can be almost any length and can contain numbers, letters, and even the underscore (_). Usually uppercase letters are used for the name of variables, but lowercase letters can be used as well. Variables can be restricted in scope to just the current process or expanded in scope to include even programs that are started by this process. User-defined variables remain defined until the user's session ends, that is, until the user logs out. Variables that you wish to have defined at all times should be defined in one of the files that will be executed when the shell program starts. These files are reviewed in the next section.

The values of all currently defined environment variables can be displayed using the **env** command as in

 env

which will list each of the currently defined variables and its value. To display the value of a particular variable you would issue the command

 echo $VAR

where "VAR" is the name of the variable of interest. For example, To display the current shell program being used, you would issue the command

 echo $SHELL

which would display the shell command being used.

In addition, each shell program recognizes a set of environment variables that modify that shell program's behavior. These variables are set by the user to control how the shell performs. A number of these variables are discussed in chapters 9 and 10 on the Korn shell and on the C shell.

A number of variables are built into the shell and these are variables that the shell itself provides. These variables can be customized for your working environment. The names of these variables are reserved for use by the shell programs.

The system administrator defines which shell program will control your terminal session. You can choose another shell program by just executing that shell program at the command line. To start the Korn shell, execute

 /bin/ksh

To start the C shell, execute

 /bin/csh

Once you do that, the new shell program will start up and be in charge of your terminal session. When you end your user session and start a new one, the shell program that was originally configured for you will, once again, be in charge of your terminal.

ESTABLISHING THE USER'S ENVIRONMENT

Each shell establishes an environment for a user when the user first logs in by executing the commands found in at least one file. The Korn shell executes both the *.kshrc* file and the *.profile* file, while the C shell executes the *.cshrc* file and the *.login* file when beginning a user session. Any command can be placed in these files to be executed when the user session begins.

Usually these files contain the definition of variables that the user will need during his or her user session. For example, if the user often executes an application that needs the *APPLDIR* variable to be defined, that variable will best be defined in one of the startup files so that the user does not need to specify it every time that user wants to run that application.

These files often contain an extensive definition of the *PATH* variable to aid in finding executables to run. You might include the directory that contains the executables that run the application that the user uses. These files also are the place to put definitions for popular commands with the options that you want.

REUSING COMMANDS EXECUTED PREVIOUSLY

Both the Korn and C shells can record commands as you execute them and then recall those commands to be edited and reexecuted. These "history" operations of the Korn and C shell programs operate much like the **DOSSHELL.EXE** program does on a DOS system—each can recall a previous command and change it.

The mechanisms for enabling the history function and recalling previous commands differ between the two shell programs and will be discussed in some detail in the next two chapters.

CREATING AND EXECUTING SHELL SCRIPTS

A shell script is a series of sequential UNIX commands that the shell program interprets and executes. In DOS systems these are called *batch* files. Just as on DOS systems, shell scripts can contain decision-making commands, looping commands, and even error handling commands. Shell scripts are created for tasks that will need to be repeated, just like batch files in DOS.

Some of the commands differ between the shell programs, but the method of creating a script is the same no matter which shell you wish to use.

The first line of a shell script should indicate under which shell to run the script. To execute the script under the C shell use

#! /bin/csh

as the first line, while to execute under the Korn shell use

#! /bin/ksh

as the first line.

You should create a subdirectory to put shell scripts into, usually called the *bin* directory, in your *HOME* directory. Now you need to set up a way for the system to find your executable scripts in that *bin* directory by changing the *PATH* variable to include your *bin* directory. For the C shell, you would code

set path = ($path $HOME/bin)

while for the Korn shell you would code

PATH=$PATH:$HOME/bin

in the appropriate script startup file.

You can give a script any name you wish, unlike DOS systems where batch files' names must end in *.BAT*. But you should not use the same name as another UNIX command because you will be confused about which command is being executed.

You create a shell script file in the *$HOME / bin* directory using **cat** or **vi** editor. You would enter each line as if you keyed that line in from the keyboard interactively. After you have created the script, you must make the script executable by changing the access permissions on the shell script using the **chmod** command as in

chmod a+x myscript

which would make the file *myscript* executable. You would then execute the shell script by entering the name of the file on the command line.

You can provide values to a script through command line arguments or environment variables as discussed earlier. Command line arguments are positional and allow arguments to be passed to a shell script. The first argument on the command line is referred to as **$1**, the second **$2**, and so on. The special variable **$#** contains the number of positional parameters with which the shell script was invoked and **$*** contains a string with all the arguments with which the shell script was invoked, starting with the first argument.

Each shell program provides a method for testing variable values and controlling operations based on other values. You can test your shell scripts and display each line as it is executed by executing the shell script with the option **vx**. For example, if you had created a script called *backup* and you want to test it out, you would execute the command

/bin/ksh -vx backup

which will execute the script *backup* and display each command before it is executed. Then when an error occurs, you will be able to determine which line in the script caused the error to occur.

Comment lines are useful in script files and are created by starting the comment with the pound sign (#) character. On UNIX systems the comment can begin anywhere on the line, while in DOS systems you would begin a line with the **rem** command in order to insert a comment into a batch file. On both UNIX and DOS systems you would display a message to the terminal using the **echo** command.

Exercises

To explore some of the common functionality of the shell programs, you should do the following:

1. Start a user session on a UNIX system. What shell program is controlling your terminal session? How do you know this? How would you change to a different shell program? What is the command line prompt? How do you know that?
2. How many shell programs exist? How many are described in

this chapter? Do other shell programs exist? Why would they exist?

3. Create a shell script to produce a list of the files in your *HOME* directory. Can you use that list to help you find a file?

4. Is there any matching facility in DOS to the UNIX shell program? What are the principal differences between UNIX shell programs and DOS shell programs?

Korn Shell Operations

OVERVIEW

The previous chapter described a number of functions provided by all UNIX shell programs. This chapter will focus on the functionality of the Korn shell that has not been discussed elsewhere in this book.

The first section of this chapter describes the interactive shell operations that the Korn shell program provides to control which directory you are in. The next section discusses how the Korn shell remembers commands and what process you would follow to recall a previous command and re-execute it after changing it. Next, some of the variables that the Korn shell recognizes and uses are described. How to define your own commands is covered in the next section. Establishing your own tailored user environment is explored, and finally, several sections describe how to use the scripting functions provided by the Korn shell program.

INTERACTIVE KORN SHELL OPERATIONS

Managing which directory you are in is one of the functions of the shell program. The **cd** command described in an earlier chapter is built into the shell program. The Korn shell remembers the most recent directory in which you were so that you can return to that directory with the command

> **cd -**

which will return you to the previous working directory. For example, suppose you had been in the */usr/marty/source* directory and you had issued the command

> **cd /usr/include**

so that you could look at one of the system header files. Now you want to return to your previous directory. You would enter the command

> **cd -**

and you would be back in the */usr/marty/source* directory.

One other shorthand method of moving to another directory provided by the Korn shell is the use of replacement strings in a **cd** command. You specify the **cd** command with the name of one of the current directories or subdirectories along with the name of the replacement directory, and the **cd** command will change to your working directory to the one requested. As an example, suppose your current working directory is */usr/marty/docs* and you wanted to change to the */usr/marty/scripts* directory, you could specify the following command:

> **cd ../scripts**

Or you could specify the command

> **cd docs scripts**

which would change you to the */usr/marty/scripts* directory. As another example, suppose you were in the */usr/spool/uucp* directory and wanted to change to the */usr/lib/uucp* directory, you would use the command

> **cd spool lib**

which would change your directory to */usr/lib/uucp*.

KORN SHELL HISTORY OPERATIONS

The Korn shell records the commands that you enter. All of these commands can be recalled, edited, and re-executed. You can even use the same editing commands that the **vi** command provides. You initiate the recording of commands by executing the command

HISTSIZE=250

which would cause the last 250 commands to be stored in a history file and become available for re-execution or editing and re-execution.

To use **vi**-like syntax to edit recorded commands you would issue the command

set -o vi

To recall a previous command, you press the **Escape** key to start the recall process. Then, each press of the character "k" will recall one previous command onto the command line where it can be edited, if desired, and then executed. Some of the commands that you can use to edit the recalled command are listed in Table 9.1. For example, suppose you have entered the command

ls -l /usr/marty

to display the contents of the */usr/marty* directory. Now you want to display the contents of one of the subdirectories in that directory, for example, the *scripts* directory. You could type in the command

ls -l /usr/marty/scripts

but you have already typed in most of this command previously. Thus, you would recall the previous command by touching the **Escape** key and then "k" to recall the most recently executed command. Now you have only to add the subdirectory in which you are interested and you can execute that command. You would do that by adding "A" to the end of the command line, typing *scripts*, and touching **Enter** to execute the command

ls -l /usr/marty/scripts

and display the contents of the subdirectory of interest. Doesn't that seem like a quicker method? This type of editing is especially useful if you have typed in a long command and misspelled or transposed letters. In this case you would recall the command, edit in the necessary changes, and then reexecute the command.

You can also recall previous commands and perform substitution on them and then execute them. This operation is performed by a special command called **fc**. Usually an alias is defined for the command **fc -e -**, called "r," so that you can enter the command

Table 9.1.   **vi** Commands to Edit Recalled Commands

Command Editing Desired	Korn Shell Command
Move left one character	l
Move right one character	h
Delete character	x
Reverse two characters	xp
Delete n words	ndw
Change n words	ncw
Replace one character	r
Add characters after current character	i
Add characters at end of line	A

> **r script=docs ls**

which will recall the most recent command that starts with "ls," will substitute "docs" for "scripts" in that command, and then will execute that modified command.

You can display the remembered commands by entering the **history** command by itself and the output might look like

```
173     ls -l utmp
174     pwd
175     who
176     env
177     set
178     alias
179     history
```

You can execute any particular command in the history list by entering the **fc** command and the number of the command to be executed. The command you just recalled will be displayed; you can then execute it by pressing the **Enter** key.

KORN SHELL VARIABLE COMMANDS

You define variables by using the equal sign (=) as in

> **GOODSTUFF=/usr/marty/docs**

But once defined, this variable is known only to the current process and needs to be **exported** to be available to any subsequent programs that are started by this shell. This is done by

> **export GOODSTUFF**

and then all subprocesses will know the value of the variable *GOODSTUFF*. One good programming practice is to combine these two commands using the semi-colon (;) operator to place two commands next to each other as one command line, as in

> **GOODSTUFF=/usr/marty/docs;export GOODSTUFF**

Using this kind of command will accomplish both the defining of the variable and its exporting so that all subsequent processes can use it. In some scripts you may desire not to **export** variables so that they are only known in the script itself.

A variable can be defined from another variable or set of variables. The syntax for such an operation requires the use of left and right curly brackets ({}) to notify the shell program of the name of the variable. For example, if you want to generate a set of file names dependent on the setting of a variable, you might code something like

> **BASE=/tmp/myfile**
> **BASE1=${BASE}1**
> **BASE2=${BASE}2**

which would create two variables whose values are */tmp/myfile1* and */tmp/myfile2*. The value to which you set a variable can be anything that you want to use later that will have meaning.

You would define multiple valued variables using the colon (:) operator. Thus, if you wanted to add another directory to an already existing definition of the *PATH* variable you would use the command

> **PATH=$PATH:/usr/marty/bin**

which would add the */usr/marty/bin* directory to the current list of directories in the *PATH* variable.

One very valuable function is the ability to capture the outcome of a command in a variable to use later. The following sets up a variable that contains the name of the current directory

      CURRENTDIR=`pwd`

by first executing the command **pwd** as requested by the backquote (`` ` ``) and then defining the variable *CURRENTDIR* to have that value.

    The command **env** will display all the environment variables currently defined, as in

      env

which would cause a display of all of the currently defined variables and their values to be shown on your terminal.

    The command **export** marks the given list of variables for export to all processes, as in

      export varname1 varname2 ...

You use the **set** command to set several of the shell's internal options and positional parameters. Without an argument, **set** displays all shell variables currently defined, as in

      set

You can delete a currently defined variable using the **unset** command, as in

      unset varname1

which would remove any definition for the variable *varname1*.

KORN SHELL BUILT-IN VARIABLES

The Korn shell recognizes a set of variables that will modify the behavior of the shell program itself. These variables are listed in Table 9.2. For example, you can specify where the shell is to look for executables with the *PATH* variable. This variable is a multi-valued variable that contains the names of directories in which to search for the executable specified on the command line. You would modify the value of the *PATH* variable with the following command

      PATH=$HOME/bin:$PATH

which would add the name of the *bin* subdirectory in the user's HOME directory to the search path for executables. The shell maintains a parallel set of variables that contain the same values.

For example, the *PATH* variable has a parallel variable called *path*. Whether you change *path* with the **set** command or *PATH* with the equal sign operator, the values will remain the same. Usually variables with names with lowercase letters are considered local variables while variables with uppercase names are considered global variables.

Another variable that the Korn shell recognizes is the *CDPATH* variable, which defines a search path for the **cd** command. This variable operates by providing a list of directories to search when looking for the directory that you have specified with the **cd** command. This is a multivalued variable just like the *path* variable.

Several other variables are useful to define. These are shown in Table 9.2. Two variables control the interaction of the shell with the mail system. The first variable, *MAIL*, defines the directory to examine for arriving mail and the second, *MAILCHECK*, defines in seconds how often to check that directory defined by the *MAIL* variable.

You can change the prompt that is displayed every time command line input is possible. You should define a prompt that contains the name of the system that you are on and the directory you are in. You would define *PS1* to be

    PS1=`uname -n`\:\$PWD[!]##

which would print the name of the system, the current working directory and the command number (plus the character "#").

In addition, a number of variables can be set to change the

Table 9.2.   Variables Used by the Korn Shell

Shell Variable	Function Provided
CDPATH	Search path for the **cd** command.
HISTSIZE	Number of commands Korn shell remembers.
MAILCHECK	How often to check for mail.
MAILPATH	Directories to monitor for modification due to *MAIL* arrival.
PATH	Directories to search for executables.
PS1	What primary command line prompt is.
SHELL	Name of shell being executed.

Table 9.3.   Variables That Modify Behavior of Korn Shell

Shell Variable User Can Modify	What Shell Variable Does
ignoreeof	Shell will not exit on end-of-file. Use **exit** command instead of **logout**.
noclobber	Prevents redirection operator (>) from truncating existing files.
noglob	Disables filename substitution.
verbose	Prints shell input lines as they are read.
xtrace	Prints commands and their arguments as they are executed.

behavior of the shell program. These variables are summarized in Table 9.3. For example, the variable *HISTSIZE* determines the number of commands stored in the history file.

CREATING YOUR OWN COMMANDS

You can define your own command using the shell subcommand **alias**. You usually set up new commands as either shorthand command names or to create a command that has the options you prefer for a command. To see what aliases are already defined, you would execute the **alias** command with no arguments, as in

    alias

which will display on your terminal all currently defined replacement commands.

To define a new command use the **alias** command followed by the name of the command to be defined with the equivalence for it, as in

    alias lf='ls -aF'

which would define the **lf** command to be the result of the execution of the command **ls -aF**. This type of command is used to specify different options for the **ls** command itself. If you wish this redefined command to be used in a script that you will invoke, you need to add the **-x** option to the **alias** command itself. You usually place the **alias** commands in the Korn shell startup file *.profile*. Two common alias commands are

> **alias -x r='fc -e -'**
> **alias -x history='fc -l'**

which will define a method for recalling a previous executed command and performing a substitution on it before executing it, and will define a method for listing the current contents of the remembered command file. Any number of **alias** commands can be defined.

Executing the **alias** command without any arguments will cause a list of the currently defined aliases to be displayed, as in

> **alias**

and the output looks like

```
autoload=typeset -fu
cat=/usr/bin/cat
false=let 0
functions=typeset -f
hash=alias -t -
history=fc -l
integer=typeset -i
nohup=nohup
r=fc -e -
stop=kill -STOP
suspend=kill -STOP $$
true=:
type=whence -v
```

You can remove a defined **alias** command with the **unalias** command.

SHELL PROGRAMMING OPERATIONS

Part of what the shell provides is a set of programming commands to enable you to create your own command sequences that perform looping and condition testing, and thus control which commands are executed under which circumstances.

Various kinds of condition testing can be used in **if** commands and **while** commands to control what operations take place. The **if** command condition testing would look like

if [condition]

with various kinds of conditions that can be tested. For example, the value of environment variables can be checked to determine which commands need to be executed or the existence of a file can be checked. These kinds of condition testing are listed in Tables 9.4 and 9.5. To gear a set of commands to the host you are using is a fairly typical activity. To perform a set of tests based on the host requires that you can determine on which host you are executing. The following code sample tests the output from the **uname** command, which will be the name of the host

```
if [ "`uname`" = "pluto" ]
then
      echo This is the pluto system
fi
```

The condition being tested in the **if** command is whether the host you are running on is *pluto*.

The **while** command uses conditions in much the same way as the **if** command, but in this case the testing is to control looping, as in

```
while [ condition ]
do
      command
end
```

which will cause the **command** command to be executed as long as *condition* is true. Conditions can be "and"ed with the **-a** operator or "or"ed with the **-o** operator to form more complex tests, as in

if [condition1 -a condition2]

which would be true if *condition1* and *condition2* were both true.

The standard if-then-else condition testing and response can be used to test variable values, for example, and based on a value perform different functions. The if-then-else construct looks like

```
if [ condition ]
then
```

Table 9.4.   Condition Tests That Can Be Performed

Test Will Be True	Operation to Perform
If length of *string* is non-zero	**-n string**
If option named *option* is on	**-o option**
If length of *string* is zero	**-z string**
If *string* matches *pattern*	**string = pattern**
If *string* does not match *pattern*	**string != pattern**
If *string1* comes before *string2* based on ASCII values	**string1 < string2**
If *string1* comes after *string2* based on ASCII values	**string1 > string2**
If *expression1* is equal to *expression2*	**expression1 -eq expression2**
If *expression1* is not equal to *expression2*	**expression1 -ne expression2**
If *expression1* is less than *expression2*	**expression1 -lt expression2**
If *expression1* is greater than *expression2*	**expression1 -gt expression2**
If *expression1* is less than or equal to *expression2*	**expression1 -le expression2**
If *expression1* is greater than or equal to *expression2*	**expression1 -ge expression2**
If *expression1* is equal to *expression2*	**expression1 -eq expression2**

Table 9.5.   File Attribute Tests That Can Be Performed

Test Will Be True	Test to Perform
If *file* exists	**-a file**
If *file* is a directory	**-d file**
If *file* exists and is ordinary	**-f file**
If *file* exists and is readable	**-r file**
If *file* exists and is more than zero bytes in length	**-s file**
If *file* exists and cannot be written	**-w file**
If *file* exists and is executable	**-x file**
If *file* exists and is a symbolic link	**-l file**
If *file* exists and is owned by owner of process	**-O file**
If *file* zero length	**-0 file**

```
    ....
else
    ....
fi
```

As an example, the following **if** command examines whether the terminal is defined as a "dialup" and prints a message indicating what kind of terminal was found:

```
if [ "$TERM" = "dialup" ]
then
    echo $TERM is dialup
else
    echo $TERM is not dialup
fi
```

Sometimes you want to examine a list of files and perform some operations on them. You can use the **find** command to generate a list of the files of interest and then you can use the **for** command to operate on them. The **for** command structure looks like

```
for a in list
do
    ....
done
```

Each item in *list* is used as the value of the *a* variable, and the commands in the *do* loop are applied to that variable. The **for** command structure ends with the **done** verb.

To use more complicated **if** command structure use the **elif** command to test another condition inside the overall **if** command. Another method to generate lists of files might be to use the **find** command, as in

```
for filename in `find /usr -name`
    do
        ....
    done
```

which will look at all the files in the */usr* directory.

One other control structure uses the **case** verb, as in

```
case $variable
in
```

```
a | b )
        ~
        ;;
c )
        ~
        ;;
* )
        ~
        ;;
esac
```

which will check the value of *variable* against the values listed in the **case** structure. If there is a match, it will perform the commands listed there. Notice that the **case** structure ends with the **esac** verb.

CONDITIONS THAT CAN BE TESTED FOR

The Korn shell provides a wide variety of conditions that can be tested, as listed in Table 9.4. One set of tests will check whether one expression is greater than, equal to, or less than another expression. Another set of tests will check string length, string values, and even if a particular option is on or off.

The shell program provides a particularly rich method for examining the attributes of a file. Table 9.5 lists a number of possible tests that you can use to check what kind of file you are examining. Each of these tests is of the form

if [-z filename]

where z is one of the letters shown in Table 9.5.

As an example, the following script looks at the files in a directory and prints out a message indicating whether the file is a "plain file."

```
for filename in *
do
if [ -f $filename ]
then
    echo $filename is a file
elif [ -d $filename ]
then
```

> **echo $filename is a directory**
> **else**
>   **echo $filename is not a file or a directory**
> **fi**
> **done**

Notice that the **for** command will loop setting the variable *filename* to each value in the list that the asterisk operator will generate.

SAMPLE KORN SHELL SCRIPT

The Korn shell script shown in Figure 9.1 will ask you a question: *Are you happy?* and comment on your answer. The two objectives of this script are to show how to ask the user a question and how to process the answer with a **case** command. The dialogue with this script will go something like

```
#!/bin/ksh
answer=" "
while [ "$answer" = " " ]
do
     echo -n "Are you happy? "
     read answer
     case $answer
     in
          y | g ) echo That\'s great\!
                    answer=" "
                    ;;
          n ) echo I\'m sorry to hear that
                    answer=" "
                    ;;
          x ) echo Tired of playing\; see you later
                    answer=" "
                    exit 1
                    ;;
          * ) echo Bad choice\; Try again
                    answer=" "
                    ;;
     esac
done
```

Figure 9.1. Script to ask a question and analyze answer.

```
Are you happy? n
I'm sorry to hear that
Are you happy? g
Bad choice; Try again
Are you happy? y
That's great!
Are you happy? x
Tired of playing; see you later
```

Notice the use of the back slash (\) in the script (see Figure 9.1) to notify the shell program that the next character is a part of the string and is not a control character.

Exercises

1. Create a directory called *bscript*. Move to directory *bscript*. Create a script to move to any other directory you have access to that will be specified on the command line, verify that you are in that other directory, and list the contents of that directory. Return to your original directory. What might that script look like?

2. Create a subdirectory in your *HOME* directory called *bin*. Move the just-created shell script to the *bin* directory. Make the shell script executable. Execute that shell script from any directory.

3. Using the history functions: Set the history facility to save 10 commands. Execute 10 commands. Look at the commands saved by the history facility. Execute the last command you entered. Execute the last **ls** command you executed. Execute the last **cd** command you executed. Execute the fifth command you executed.

C Shell Operations

OVERVIEW

Chapter 8 described many functions common to all shell programs. This chapter will focus on the functionality provided by the C shell. The first part of this chapter discusses interactive shell operations that control what directory you are in and the history mechanism that enables you to recall and re-execute previously executed commands. Next, we examine how to define shell variables and which shell variables the C shell uses. Lastly, the chapter discusses how to program using C shell commands and what conditions can be tested for.

INTERACTIVE C SHELL OPERATIONS

Managing which directory you are in is one of the functions of the shell program. The **cd** command described in an earlier chapter is built into the shell program. The C shell program provides several other commands to aid in moving from directory to directory.

The command **pushd** will change your working directory to a new one and, in addition, will record what directory you have just left. The **popd** command will change your working directory to the previous one in the list of directories that you created with the **pushd** commands. For example, if you are in the */usr/marty* directory and you execute

pushd docs

your working directory will become */usr/marty/docs* and your list of directories will be

```
/usr/marty/docs
/usr/marty
```

If you were to now execute

pushd ../scripts

your working directory would become */usr/marty/scripts* and your directory list would be

```
/usr/marty/scripts
/usr/marty/docs
/usr/marty
```

You can return to either of the previous directories just by issuing the **popd** command.

The pairing of the commands **pushd** and **popd** enables scripts to be written that will execute in a particular directory and return to the directory from which the script was called. This use of the pair of commands will be discussed in a later section of this chapter.

On some UNIX systems the C shell can be requested to check the spelling of the directory to which you want to change. If the directory does not exist, the C shell will try to find a directory that is closest in name to the one that you originally requested. The C shell will interrogate you to determine if you want to change to this directory and if you choose to do so, will change you to that directory.

C SHELL HISTORY OPERATIONS

The C shell will record every command that you execute. This history facility can be used to remember any previous command and re-execute it or to recall a previous command and edit it.

Even any argument in a previous command can be reused in a subsequent command.

To simply re-execute the previous command without editing it, you would use the !! operator. Thus, if you had entered the command

cd ..

to move up one directory and you wanted to move up another, you would just enter

!!

The previous command would be re-executed and you would move up another directory. You can add to the end of the command when you re-execute it by following the !! operator with whatever string you wish to add. For example, if you had entered the command

ls /usr/marty

to see the contents of the /usr/marty directory and you wanted to examine the docs subdirectory in that directory, you would use the command

!!/docs

which would examine the /usr/marty/docs directory. The important point is that you did not need to retype the /usr/marty string.

To edit the previous command, use the caret (^) operator to specify what change to make to the previous command. When using this substitution operator, specify first the field you want to substitute for and then the field to be substituted. For example, if instead of the docs subdirectory you wanted to examine the scripts subdirectory, you would issue the command

^docs^scripts

and the command

ls /usr/marty/scripts

would be issued and the contents of the /usr/marty/scripts directory would be displayed on the terminal.

Each command in the history list can be referred to by a sequential event number. The history list can be displayed by using the **history** command. You can execute a particular previous command by using the exclamation mark (!) operator with the number of the command. For example, after issuing the commands shown earlier and you executed the **history** command, the output might look like

```
21 cd ..
22 cd ..
23 ls /usr/marty
24 ls /usr/marty/docs
25 ls /usr/marty/scripts
```

showing (in this example) the last five commands you executed. The full command is recorded, not the shorthand method of invoking it. The number of commands that are remembered is determined by the value of the *history* variable. If you want to issue command number 24 again, you would enter the command

!24

If you wanted to issue the most recent command that contained the string *docs*, you could use the exclamation point operator again with a question mark as in

!?docs

which would re-execute the last command that contained the string *docs* in it.

Other more complicated editing of the previous command on the history list can be done with the *:s* operator. For example, if you wanted to execute command number 23, but for the subdirectory *jsmith*, you would enter the command

!23:s/marty/jsmith

and the contents of the */usr/jsmith* directory would be displayed on your terminal. One useful way to use the history list is to recall just one of the arguments in a previous command. You refer to an argument in the previous command by number starting with 0 (zero), which refers to the command itself. Thus if you had entered the command

cp /usr/marty/scripts/* /usr/jsmith

and you wanted to display the contents of the */usr/jsmith* directory, you could enter the command

ls !!:2

which means list the contents of the directory that is the second
argument in the previous command. To recall a previous command and just display it (to see what it was), you would use the *:p*
operator as in

!24:p

which would display on your terminal

```
ls /usr/marty/docs
```

You can now use that command just as if it had been the previous
command that you entered at the terminal.

Other command editing operations exist but they are somewhat
dependent on the particular UNIX system on which you are executing. You should examine the manual page for the **csh** command to
see what other editing options are available on your system.

C SHELL VARIABLE COMMANDS

You define a variable using the **setenv** command as in

setenv VARIABLE1 value_of_variable1

which defines the variable *VARIABLE1* to equal the value
value_of_variable1. You would refer to the value of *VARIABLE1*
by placing a dollar sign in front of the name of the variable that
you have defined. Thus, if you define a set of directories of interest as in

setenv SUBS /usr/marty/source/appl1/subs
setenv WORK /usr/marty/work/appl1
setenv DATA /usr/marty/data/appl1
setenv INCLUDE /usr/marty/include/appl1

and you wanted to see the contents of the *WORK* directory, you
would only have to enter the command

ls $WORK

and the contents of the */usr/marty/work/appl1* directory would be displayed on your terminal. You can refer to these variables in any command such as

cp $SUBS/*.h $INCLUDE

to copy files from one directory to another.

You can use the **set** command to modify some of the C shell's built-in variables. For example, executing the command

set history=250

will cause the C shell to remember 250 commands. This type of command could be placed in the user's startup command (See "Creating Your Own Commands" later in this chapter).

You can create a multivalued variable with the command

set path=(/usr/local /usr/bin /bin /etc \.)

which would define the *path* variable to contain the names of several directories. The *path* variable is used by the shell program to locate executable programs. The parentheses indicate that you are defining a multivalued variable. If you did not include parentheses and issued the command

set path= /usr/local /usr/bin /bin /etc \.

you would define the variable *path* to have the single value */usr/local /usr/bin /bin /etc* \. You can determine the number of values that the multivalued variable contains by using the command

echo $#path

which will indicate the number of values for this multivalued variable. You can refer to a particular entry in a multivalued variable using square brackets ([]), as in

echo $path[3]

to display the third value in the multivalued variable named *path*.

You can set the value of a variable with the value that a command returns by using the backward single quote (`) operator. As an example, the command

setenv port `tty`

which will create a variable called *port* that contains the name of the device that you are using to attach to the host. If the value returned by the command that you executed contains more than one value separated by a blank or a new line, then the variable can be defined as one long string variable or a multivalued variable. Try the following command

set jobs_to_kill=(`ps -ef | grep marty`)

which will create a multivalued variable with the fields from the **ps** command. Now try the following commands:

echo $#jobs_to_kill
echo $jobs_to_kill[1]
echo $jobs_to_kill[4]

which will display first the number of arguments in the *jobs_to_kill* variable and then some of the entries in that multivalued variable. Unfortunately, this method of producing the list also produces a large number of output fields that are not useful in trying to stop all the processes that belong to *marty*.

You can display all currently defined environment variables using the **env** command. You can display the value of a specific variable using the **echo** command, as in

echo $VARIABLE1

which will display the current value of the variable *VARIABLE1*. The **echo** command will display both variables that are defined with the **set** command and those variables defined with the **setenv** command. You can display the value of all of the shell variables by using the **set** command.

You remove the definition of a variable defined with the **set** command with the **unset** command, as in

unset variable-name

You can remove the definition of a variable defined with the **setenv** command with the **unsetenv** command, as in

unsetenv variable-name

which will delete that variable from the list of known variables.

C SHELL BUILT-IN VARIABLES

The C shell examines a number of variables to determine its behavior. These variables can be modified by the user to change the behavior of the C shell. Table 10.1 lists these variables and shows the effect that changing them will have. In addition, the shell program provides a number of variables that contain valuable information that a user can use but not change. These are listed in Table 10.2. For example, the shell program will find an executable for you if you indicate in the *path* variable in which directories the shell program should look for an executable. To define the *path* variable, for example, you might try something like

set path = ($HOME/bin $path)

which will add the directory *$HOME/bin* to the current list of directories to search for executables. Now the shell will also look

Table 10.1.   User Modifiable C Shell Variables

Shell Variables User Can Modify	What Shell Variable Does
echo	If set, each command and its arguments are echoed before being executed.
history	Number of commands in history list.
ignoreeof	If set, ^D does not terminate shell.
mail	Files where shell checks for mail. If first word is numeric, specifies how often to check for new mail (in seconds).
noclobber	If set, files are not overwritten without specific instructions.
nonomatch	If set, it is not an error for a filename expansion not to match any existing files.
path	Directories in which to search for commands to be executed.
prompt	String printed each time a new command is expected from terminal.
term	Describes what type of terminal on which you are entering commands.
verbose	If set, each command is displayed before substitution is performed.

Table 10.2.   Read-Only C Shell Variables

Shell Variables User Cannot Modify	What Shell Variable Does
home	Home directory of shell invoker
shell	Name of shell under which you are executing
status	Status returned by last command
user	Name of user
$$	Process number of the shell program

in the *$HOME/bin* directory for executables. You can insert the current directory in the *path* variable with

set path = ($path \.)

Remember that you are specifying the order of the search so that if an executable is found in more than one directory, the one that will be executed is the one that is found first using the *path* variable.

One special purpose variable is the *$$* variable, which the C shell will set to the process id of the C shell process itself. This variable can be used to construct temporary filenames that will be unique, even if a script is being run simultaneously by two different users. As an illustration, consider the following script operation:

find . -print | grep "\.o" > /tmp/object.list

which will generate a list of files whose names end in ".o", that is, files that are object files. You might do this if you are building a library of object files and then you want to delete those object files. If two users were to execute this script at the same time, each would create the same file named */tmp/object.list*, but one user would be disappointed with its contents. You can cause the script to create files that are uniquely named by using the built-in variable *$$* as in the following example

find . -print | grep "\.o" > /tmp/obj$$.list

which will cause each script to create its own unique file. To end the user session, you can choose to specify that the user must enter the **exit** command and not just the **^D** command. To do this you would define the variable *ignoreeof* as in

set ignoreeof

which sets the value of *ignoreeof* to 1.

The directory in which your user session starts is called the *HOME* directory. This variable is defined by the shell program itself and should not be changed.

You can specify in what directory your mail will arrive so that you can be notified when new mail arrives for you. You can define this by

set mail = (# mailfilepath)

which defines how often to check for new mail and the name of the directory (or directories) that should be observed for new mail.

Several variables are predefined when the C shell starts. The variable *shell* or *SHELL* will contain the fully qualified name of the shell program you are executing. The variables *home* and *HOME* will contain the directory that has been defined as your home directory.

CREATING YOUR OWN COMMANDS

You can define your own commands using the **alias** command. You should create commands for the common operations that you do. For example, if there are particular options that you always use with a command, you should create a command of your own that specifies those options. For example, if you always want to use the **-aF** option of the **ls** command, you should create an alias for the **ls** command that contains those options. The command

alias ls ls -aF

would define your own version of the **ls** command that includes the **-aF** options. This **ls** command would operate just like the original. For compatibility with DOS systems, you might want a command **dir** that displayed a listing of the contents of the directory. The command

alias dir ls -aF

would do exactly that.

Another use of the **alias** command is to create shorthand ways of executing commands. For example, the following will create abbreviations for **finger** and **telnet**

alias f finger
alias t telnet

You can create 26 single letter commands and even 10 single number commands to use.

The name of the command that you define can be the same as the name of another command. The only issue will be remembering how your version compares to the real command. If one of your UNIX systems does not have quite the same name for a command as another, you can create an alias for that command so that you only have to remember one command name and not two. For example, you might want to have a definition for the DOS command **DIR** so that when you are on a UNIX system, you do not have to constantly remember that this is the **ls** command. To define aliases for **DIR** and **dir** commands, you would issue the command

alias DIR ls -l
alias dir ls -l

You should add these definitions permanently to your user environment.

You can determine what aliases are defined by using the **alias** command by itself, as in

alias

which would produce output like

```
cd      (chdir !$ ; set prompt=`uname -n`\:`pwd`\[\!\]%\ )
dir     (ls -aF)
l       (ls -l)
ls      (ls -aF)
DIR     (ls -l)
```

which lists the currently defined aliases and their definitions. Your own list of aliases would be different.

SHELL PROGRAMMING OPERATIONS

You can perform looping, condition testing, and so on in a shell script. Script files are created with a text editor and operate much the same way that the DOS batch files operate. One difference is that UNIX shell scripts can be named almost anything, but DOS batch files must end in *.BAT*. Another difference is that the C shell script language is much richer than the DOS batch command language.

The conditional clauses use the **if - then - else - endif** command structure as in the following

```
if ( condition )
then
    ~
else
    ~
endif
```

which will use the value of *condition* to determine whether the commands in the **then** section or in the **else** section will be executed.

The C shell program provides both the **while** command and the **foreach** command to perform looping operations. For example, the following **while** loop will be executed five times:

```
i=0
while ( i < 5 )
    i++
    echo i = $i
end
```

As an example of the use of the **foreach** structure, examine the following script, which will list the names of the files in the */usr/marty/scripts* directory

```
foreach file ( /usr/marty/scripts/* )
    echo File found is $file
    echo "----------------------------"
end
```

In the **while - end** and the **foreach - end** structures, any valid command can be used in these structures, including **while** and **foreach**.

You can also test the value of a variable and process some of the possible values with a **switch - case - end** command structure.

```
switch $VARIABLE
    case "value1":
        command1
        break
    case "value2":
        command2
        break
    default
end
```

As an example of the use of the **switch** command, examine the following commands (usually placed in the *.cshrc* file):

```
switch `uname -a`
    case "host1"
        setenv WORK /usr/work
        break
    case "host2"
        setenv WORK /usr/lib/work
        break
    default
        setenv WORK /usr/var/work
end
```

which will use the output of the command **uname -a** to cause certain commands to be executed only on certain systems. In this way, you can have just one *.cshrc* file and manage differences among several hosts.

Changing the value of a variable in a script executed from the command line does not change the value of the variable outside of the script.

CONDITIONS THAT CAN BE TESTED FOR

You can test the value of an environment variable by using the compare operators: "==", "!=", "<=", ".=", ">", or "<". For example, to test whether the value of the variable *VAR1* is "abcd," you would code

if ($VAR1 == "abcd")

Note that this syntax is very much like the C language syntax. To test whether *VAR1* is defined at all, you would use the test

if ($?VAR1)

which will return "1" if the variable is defined and "0" if it is not. Thus, the command structure

if ($?variable)
then
    ~
else
    ~
endif

would cause the commands in the **then** clause to be executed if it is defined and the commands in the **else** clause to be executed if it is not. One variable whose existence is worth testing for is the **prompt** variable. If it is defined, you know that you are running in an interactive session. If it is not defined, you know you are executing a script. For example,

if ($?prompt) then
    set hn = `hostname`
    if (`whoami` != "root") then
        set prompt = "$hn% "
    else
        set prompt = "$hn# "
    endif
    set history = 120
endif

will set up the prompt to show the hostname and the command number only if the *prompt* variable is defined.

You can test the attributes of a file by using the following form of the **if** command

if (-l filename)

where "l" is one of the arguments listed in Table 10.3. Thus, you can check whether a file even exists with the test

Table 10.3.   C Shell File Attribute Tests

Test Desired	Option to Use
Does file exist?	**e**
Is file a plain file?	**f**
Is file of zero length?	**z**
Is file a directory?	**d**
Is file readable by user?	**r**
Is file writable by user?	**w**
Is file executable by user?	**x**

> **if (-e /a/b/c)**

which would be true if the file existed and false if it did not. Another test can be performed to test whether the file is readable by the executor of the script. You can combine these condition tests together using the or (| |) operator or the and (&&) operator. Thus, the **if** command

> **if ($VAR1 > 0 && $VAR1 < 10)**

would be true if the value of *$VAR1* was between zero and ten.

As another example, the following code displays a message if the file does not exist or if the file is not a read file:

```
if ( -e /a/b/c ) && ( -f /a/b/c )
then
     echo /a/b/c is an existing plain file
else
     echo /a/b/c doesn't exist and
     echo /a/b/c is not a plain file
endif
```

You should test all the necessary conditions for the various files that you will need to execute your scripts.

SAMPLE C SHELL SCRIPTS

The sample script shown in Figure 10.1 illustrates a method of asking the user for some information and then analyzing the response that was received. The example uses the **while** com-

```
#!/bin/csh
setenv answer " "
while ( "$answer" == " " )
     echo -n "Are you happy? "
     setenv answer $<
     switch ( $answer )
          case "y":
               echo That\'s great\!
               breaksw
          case "n":
               echo I\'m sorry to hear that
               breaksw
          default:
               echo Bad choice\; Try again
               setenv answer " "
               breaksw
     endsw
end
```

Figure 10.1.   Script to ask a question and analyze answer.

mand to ask repeatedly for an answer and the **switch** command
to analyze the answer that was given.

The sample script shown in Figure 10.2 illustrates one tech-
nique for examining a list of files. This example only tests some of
the attributes of each of the entries on the list of files to deter-

```
#!/bin/csh -f
foreach filename ( * )
     if ( -f $filename ) then
          echo $filename is a file
     else if ( -d $filename ) then
          echo $filename is a directory
     else
          echo $filename is not a file and
          echo $filename is not a directory
     endif
end
```

Figure 10.2.   Script to examine a set of files.

mine whether that file is a directory, plain file, or neither. This example thus demonstrates how to use the special attribute tests shown in Table 10.1. The metacharacter asterisk (*) is used to develop a list of files. This method of generating a file list could be replaced by some other method such as

foreach filename (*.c)

which produces a list that contains only files whose name ends in ".c". Other methods of producing lists of items can be used as long as the entries in the list are separated by blanks or new lines. To find files that satisfy other qualifications you can use the **find** command to develop that list of files.

You can even use a list of objects that are in a text file. In that case you would use the command

foreach filename (`cat textfile`)

to pass the contents of the *textfile* to the **foreach** command for use in the loop. For example, you can manage your own mailing lists by creating a mailing list with the names of the users to which you want to send particular messages. Now when you want to send a message to that mailing list, you would use a script like

```
foreach name (`cat maillist`)
    echo Sending a letter to $name
    mail $name < letter
end
```

which will mail the *letter* file to each of the names in the *maillist* file.

Exercises

1. Set the history facility to save 10 commands. Execute 10 commands. Look at the commands saved by the history facility. Execute the last command you entered. Execute the last **ls** command you executed. Execute the last **cd** command you executed. Execute the fifth command you executed.
2. Create a directory called *cscript*. Move to directory *cscript*. Create the *bin* subdirectory in your home directory. Add the *bin* subdirectory to your *PATH* variable.

3. Create a script to move to any other directory you have access to, which you specify on the command line, verify that you are in that other directory, list the contents of that directory, and return to the original directory. Move the just-created shell script to the *bin* directory. Make the shell script executable. Execute that shell script from any directory.

11

Sending and Receiving Messages

OVERVIEW

One of the first tasks that UNIX was created to do was to enable two users to communicate with each other without the recipient of the message currently being on the system. This operation is called *electronic mail* and its functions are provided in UNIX systems with the **mail** command. In the DOS world, a number of packages can be purchased that provide a friendly user interface for reading and sending mail. Unfortunately for the UNIX world, the **mail** command is not very user-friendly, but provides relatively similar functionality.

Two different messaging functions need to be performed: reading mail sent to you and sending mail to others. Just like the **vi** command, **mail** is a bimodal command, you are either in *insert* mode to create a message or in *command* mode to read your messages. Both of these topics will be addressed in this chapter.

READING YOUR MESSAGES

Other users can correspond with you even if you are not currently on the system by sending you mail. When you sign onto the system, you will be notified if there is mail for you with the message

```
You have mail
```

Now you can read the mail others have sent you by entering the **mail** command, as in

mail

which gives you a list of the messages that you have not yet read, as in

```
System V Mail Type ? for help.
"/usr/spool/mail/martya": 1 message 1 new
>N  1 martya  Tue Nov 30 10:01  11/262   Good News
```

which indicates that you have one message. If you have no messages to read, the **mail** command will exit with the message

```
No mail in /usr/spool/mail/martya.
```

You can read your messages in succession just by touching the **Enter** key; the oldest unread message will be displayed. Thus, if you just touch the **Enter** key, you will have displayed

```
Message 1:
From martya Tue Nov 30 10:01:24 1993
From: martya@major.UUCP (Martin R. Arick ext 4892)
X-Mailer: SCO System V Mail (version 3.2)
To: martya
Subject: Good News
Date: Tue, 30 Nov 93 10:01:20 EST
Message-ID:  <9311301001.aa05580@major.UUCP>
Status: R

hello from me

Marty
```

If you now wish to end the reading of your messages, you would enter the command

quit

and the following messages would appear

```
Saved 1 message in /u/martya/mbox
Held 0 messages in /usr/spool/mail/martya.
```

indicating that you had read all of the new messages and none were left in your mailbox. Any messages that you had not yet read will be saved for you and you can read them later.

For any particular message there are several operations that you can perform. These are summarized in Table 11.1. The **mail** command is case sensitive; thus, the command **f** means to save the message, and the command **F** means to forward the message. The subcommand **s** will save the message to a file, and the subcommand **d** will delete the message. Messages are numbered. You can refer to a message by its number. Thus, for example, if you wanted to save the message you had just read, you would enter the command

s 1 save

and the message

```
"save" [New file] 11/272
```

would be displayed indicating that the message was saved in the file named *save*.

The current message can be referred to by a dot (.), while the dollar sign ($) is the last message, and asterisk (*) is all messages. Most of the **mail** subcommands will operate on a list of messages. A range of message numbers can be specified by using a hyphen (-) to designate a range of message numbers. Thus,

n-m

is an inclusive list of messages from number n to number m.

Two **mail** operations of particular significance are **f** (forward the message) and **r** (reply to the message that has been received). When forwarding a message, you will be asked to provide the name of the person to whom you wish this message to be sent. When replying to a message, you will placed in input mode so you can create your reply message. When you finish composing your reply, you will be asked if there are any people to receive this message by sending them a carbon copy ("cc:").

You can save the message to a file using the **s** command. As

Table 11.1. Subcommands of the **mail** Command

Mail Operation	Abbr	What Mail Operation Does
delete [msglist]	d	Delete message from mailbox
forward [msgnum] user1	f	Forward message to *user1*
respond [msgnum] user1		Respond to message with a message of your own
save [msgnum] filename	s	Save message(s) in *filename*
type [msgnum]	t	Print message on terminal
next	n	Display next message
mail user		Send a mail to *user*
quit	q	Quit, leaving messages unread
xit	e	Quit, saving messages
header	h	Display list of active messages
top [msglist]		Display first five lines of message
!		Execute shell command
list	l	Display all commands
?		Display explanations of commands

Note: [msglist] is optional and specifies messages by number, author, subject or type. The default is the current message.

part of the **s** command you would enter the name of the file in which to store the mail message.

SENDING A MESSAGE TO ANOTHER USER

To send mail to a user, you merely need to execute the **mail** command and specify the name of the person to whom you want to send a message on the command line as an option, as in

mail harry

which would start the **mail** command to create a message to send to the user *harry*. The cursor will be placed at the beginning of the next line but no prompt will be shown there. The **mail** command is waiting for you to type in your message. You can type in as long a message as you wish. When the message is complete, you indicate that fact to the **mail** command by pressing the **Control** key and the **d** key at the beginning of a line.

Following the creation of your mail message, the **mail** command will prompt for whom to send carbon copies to with the "cc:" prompt. You can enter no names by pressing **Enter** or just one name by typing that name in, or you could enter several names by stringing them on the same line separated by commas.

The person to whom you have sent a message does not have to be logged onto the system. In fact, the person might actually be on a different host somewhere in your network. To send a message to such a person, you need to put the name of the host as part of the name of the person to whom the letter is addressed. The format of this network addressing is

harry@jbm.com

which would send the mail to the host *jbm.com* and deliver the mail to the user *harry* who is expected to be reading his mail there. In fact, user *harry* could be reading his mail somewhere else. As long as the host *jbm.com* knows how to forward mail to *harry*, your message will be delivered. If the address that you specify is not correct, the letter will be returned to you as an "Undeliverable message." If you specified the above address as just *harry*, the mail delivery system will expect to deliver the mail locally.

You can put a subject on your message by using the **-s** command option. This information is then displayed in the one line entry that you saw when you looked at your messages that you received from others. For example, the command

mail -s "Greetings from your pal SNOOPY" harry

will send mail to the user *harry* and indicate that the subject is just a "Greetings" message. The **mail** command will then place you in input mode so that you can type in the message for *harry*. You should use as a subject something that will catch the user's attention and indicate whether this message needs to be read immediately or not. You probably would get a different response from "harry" if you sent a message as in

mail -s "Your printer is on fire" harry

which would probably cause *harry* to check what his printer was doing. A message is not necessary; you can use the subject as your message. You are not required to type in a message if you do not wish to. As another example, suppose you are trying to schedule a meeting. You might use the following command

mail -s "Operations mtg is 4PM Tuesday"
harry,fred,janice

The **mail** command will expect you to type in a message but you can just press **Control** and **D** keys together and an empty message will be sent to each name on your list. The subject field contains the message so no message is needed.

After you enter the **mail** command with the names of the users, you will be placed in the input mode, and every character that you type will be inserted into the message. Each line can be edited using the backspace key, but once the **Enter** key has been pressed, the line can no longer be edited. When your message is complete, you can send it by pressing **Control-D**. But suppose that you need to change the message before you send it. You can edit the entire message by using a tilde (~) command to start up an editor. You can even use one of the tilde commands to insert a file into the message that you are creating. These tilde commands are subcommands of the **mail** command and are listed in Table 11.2 with a short description for each subcommand. As an example, suppose that you have issued the command

mail marick

and replied to the prompt

```
Subject: Bad News
```

and then entered the following lines of text to be in the message to send to *marick*

```
THis is not so good news.
Marty
```

At this point you decide that you need to change the message. You want to edit the message and at least indicate what the "Bad

Table 11.2.   Tilde Commands in Input Mode of **mail** Command

Tilde Commands	What Tilde Command Does
~!shell-command	Execute "shell-command" and return.
~.	Halt message input.
~?	Print a summary of tilde commands.
~b name ...	Add the *name(s)* to the blind carbon copy (bcc) list.
~!^c name ...	Add the *name(s)* to the carbon copy (cc) list.
~d	Read in the *dead.letter* file.
~h	Prompt for "Subject" and "To," "cc," "bcc" lists.
~M [msglist]	Insert the specified messages into the letter, with no indentation.
~m [msglist]	Insert the specified messages into the letter, shifting the new text to the right one tab stop.
~p	Print the message being entered.
~q	Quit from input mode by simulating an interrupt.
~r filename	Read in the specified file.
~s string	Set the subject line to *string*.
~t name ...	Add the *name(s)* to the "To" list.
~v	Invoke a preferred screen editor on the partial message.
~w filename	Write the partial message onto *filename* file without the header.

News" is. You probably want to correct "THis" also. To do that you would invoke the editor with the tilde subcommand

> **~v**

which will create a temporary file with your message in it and then start the **vi** editor to edit that message. Once you have the **vi** editor started, you can make any changes to the message that you wish. After you are finished you will save the file with the usual **vi** command

> **ZZ**

and you will get the messages

```
"/tmp/Re5589" 3 lines, 32 characters
(continue)
```

You can now add more to the message or mail it with the usual command pressing **Control-D**.

You can also create a message with a text editor (such as the **vi** editor) and pass it into the **mail** command, as in:

mail harry < letter_to_harry

where the file *letter_to_harry* contains the message that you want to send *harry*. Creating the message before using the **mail** command to send it allows you to make sure that you have included all of the information that you wished and in the order in which you wanted to put it.

Exercises

The following lab exercise is to get you to explore the various functions of the **mail** command.

1. Send yourself a message using the **mail** command.
2. Use the **mail** command to read your message.
3. Delete the message.
4. Send a message to someone who is not logged into the system. Where has that message gone? How does the person who is not logged on the system know to read their mail?
5. Have a friend send you a message.
6. Send a message to one of the people logged in to the system. How does that person know to read your message?
7. Create a mail message to some fictitious user by first typing in a message and then editing it using the appropriate tilde command. Now use the "To" subcommand option to send that message to yourself. What will happen to the mail message to the fictitious user?
8. Read your mail and dismiss it. Did using a subject help you?
9. Create a letter in a file. Mail that letter to yourself.
10. Read your mail and save it in a file. Compare that file with the original letter that you created. Why are they different?
11. Do you have any friends on the Internet? Send a message to one of them. Why is the name of the user not enough to deliver mail to?

12

Working with Diskettes

OVERVIEW

UNIX systems have numerous commands to accomplish specific operations. This chapter will discuss commands that are useful but did not seem to fit into any other chapter in this book. For example, existing commands that will transfer files from a DOS system to a UNIX system are discussed here. We will also examine commands that write files onto diskettes and read files from diskettes.

TRANSFERRING FILES FROM UNIX TO DOS

Files that are currently stored on UNIX systems may need to be moved to DOS systems and vice versa. In the previous chapter we discussed how to accomplish this transfer using network commands, but what if the DOS system is not logically or physically connected to the UNIX system? How would we transfer files between the two of them? Many UNIX systems have diskette drives, and a diskette could provide a physical medium that could be read on a DOS system as well. But what format would we use on diskettes? An earlier section discussed using the **tar** command to store files on diskettes, but unfortunately, the format of the diskettes produced by the **tar** command is not usually readable on a DOS system.

To solve the problem of moving files physically from a UNIX system to a DOS system and back, a number of UNIX systems provide commands designed specifically to move files from a DOS-formatted diskette to the UNIX system and back. These commands differ from UNIX system to UNIX system. On one popular UNIX system, the command to transfer files from UNIX to DOS or vice versa is called **doscp**; on another system, similarly functioning commands are called **dosread** and **doswrite**. Either of these commands is used for the same purposes—to move files from a DOS-formatted diskette into a UNIX system or from a UNIX system onto a DOS-formatted diskette. Once the file is on a DOS-formatted diskette, that diskette can be physically taken to the DOS system of interest and the usual DOS commands can be used to access the diskette.

You can format the diskette in the DOS format with the **dosformat** command, as in

> **dosformat a:**

which will format the diskette in a DOS-formatted style that can be read on a DOS system.

On one particular UNIX system, to copy a file from a UNIX system onto a DOS-formatted diskette, you would use the command **doscp** as in

> **doscp file1 a:**

which requests copying of *file1* onto the diskette in drive A. The definition of a diskette drive as "A" is the responsibility of the UNIX system administrator. The specification of the diskette drive name can also be replaced with the actual device name, such as */dev/rfd0*. Once the file is on the diskette, you can check the diskette's contents by using the **dosdir** command, as in

> **dosdir a:**

which will list the contents of the diskette in the "A" drive.

All of these commands to copy files onto DOS diskettes or from DOS diskettes have several limitations. The first is that filenames are much more restrictive on DOS systems than on UNIX systems. Thus, the command

> **doscp file_to_copy.good a:**

will cause the filename to be *file_to_.goo* on the DOS diskette. In fact, if you copied a second file as in

> **doscp file_to_copy1.good a:**

you would end up overwriting the original file that you copied. A second limitation is that wildcards cannot be used to specify which file to retrieve off of the DOS diskette. Thus, the command

> **doscp a:*.* .**

will fail with the error *file not found*.

One other consideration when moving files from DOS systems to UNIX systems or from UNIX to DOS is that on DOS systems each line in an ASCII text file is terminated with both a linefeed and a carriage return, while in UNIX systems lines in ASCII files are terminated only with a linefeed. The **doscp** command will make the appropriate conversion of linefeed/carriage return to linefeed if you so desire. For the **doscp** command, the conversion is automatic and must be turned off if you do not desire it. Thus, the command

> **doscp file_to_copy.good a:**

will cause the *file_to_copy.good* to be copied to the diskette in the "A" drive and all linefeeds found in the file will be converted to carriage return/linefeed. In addition, on DOS systems files end with the control character "^Z," while there is no file-ending character on UNIX systems. So in addition to converting carriage return/linefeeds, **doscp** will also either add a "^Z" or remove a "^Z," depending on which type of system is the target system.

READING AND WRITING FILES ONTO REMOVABLE MEDIA

UNIX systems generally store files on removable media such as diskettes to save them for future use or so that these files can be moved to another system. Software that is to be installed on a

UNIX system will often arrive on a diskette. DOS systems often use the same approach: diskettes contain the software that will be installed. The DOS **copy** command may be used to move a file from a diskette into a system, as in

copy a:some.exe c:\appl\bin

which would copy the executable *some.exe* to the directory *c:\appl\bin*.

UNIX systems provide the **tar** command to store files on diskettes or tapes. The **tar** command will store files from any directory or subdirectory and will preserve the directory structure if you wish. The output from the **tar** command is usually called a "tar image" file because the **tar** command specially formats its output file. The traditional method of using the **tar** command is to store files on a removable medium such as a diskette or tape, but the **tar** command will also store files into a file on disk. In fact, you can combine the **tar** and **compress** commands to create a file that contains a number of files in it already compressed for transfer. These two commands combined can be used to imitate the operation of the DOS-based **pkzip/pkunzip** commands.

In the simplest use of the **tar** command, you can store the *file1* file on a diskette with the command

tar cvf /dev/rfd0 file1

Notice that the **tar** command does not require the hyphen like most UNIX commands. The command line option **cvf** indicates that you want to **c**reate a tar image, display **v**erbose output while doing it, and that the next command line argument will be the name of the **f**ile on which to store the tar image output file. In this example, the next command line argument is */dev/rfd0*, which is the name of the first diskette drive on the system. All the rest of the arguments on the command line are expected to be the names of files or directories, whose contents will be copied to the tar image output file.

Before you can use a diskette for a tar image, that diskette must be properly formatted. You would do that with the command

format /dev/rfd0

which is the same command as you would use in DOS to format a diskette. The formatting of this diskette for UNIX systems is different from the format of a DOS diskette. Once this diskette has been formatted in the UNIX system format, it can be used on any UNIX system, but not on a DOS system.

As another example of the **tar** command, you would issue the command

   tar cvf /dev/rfd0 file1 docs

to store the contents of the *file1* file and the *docs* directory on a diskette. You can retrieve a particular file from the diskette with the command

   tar xvf /dev/rfd0 file1

which will extract the *file1* file from the diskette and place it into the current directory. If no specific file is requested, all the files in the tar image output file will be extracted and placed in the current directory.

One very useful feature of the **tar** command is that it will preserve the directory structure on diskette that the files had on disk. For example, referring to the directory layout shown in Figure 3.1, if you are in the *usr/marty* directory and execute the command

   tar cvf /dev/rfd0 *

all of the files in the directory *marty* will be stored on the diskette, as well as all of the files in the *docs* subdirectory and all of the files in the *scripts* subdirectory as well. In addition, the subdirectory in which each of the files was will be recorded as well. The output from this command would be

```
a docs
a docs/manual1 9 blocks
a docs/manual2 15 blocks
a file1 83 blocks
a memos1 9 blocks
a scripts
a scripts/chkfiles 3 blocks
a scripts/doit 1 blocks
```

preserving the subdirectory structure of the *marty* directory. Each block is a maximum of 512 bytes long. When you restore the files from the diskette, the directory structure will be recreated exactly as it existed in the original directory */usr/marty*.

You can verify which files you have stored on the diskette by executing the command

tar tvf /dev/rfd0

which will list the table of contents of the diskette as

```
drwxrwxrwx 378 55     0 Nov 01 10:48:59 1993 docs/
-rw-rw-rw- 378 55  4899 Nov 01 10:48:59 1993 docs/manual1
-rwxr-xr-x 378 55  7046 Jul 19 14:06:04 1993 docs/manual2
-rwxr-xr-x 378 55 41478 Jul 19 14:06:04 1993 file1
-rwxr-xr-x 378 55  4278 Jul 18 14:07:04 1993 memos1
drwxrwxrwx 378 55     0 Jul 17 13:06:04 1993 scripts/
-rwxr-xr-x 378 55  1278 Jul 19 13:06:04 1993 scripts/chkfiles
-rwxr-xr-x 378 55   478 Jul 19 13:06:04 1993 scripts/doit
```

Notice that the subdirectory name is stored on the diskette as well as the name of the files. In addition, the access permissions, owner, group owner, and date of last modification are also recorded when the tar image output file is created. These files could then be copied from this diskette into a different directory and the **tar** command will create any subdirectories that are needed. As an example, if you changed to the */tmp* directory and executed the command

tar xvf /dev/rfd0

you will see the output

```
x docs
x docs/manual1 5 blocks
x docs/manual2 4 blocks
x file1 4 blocks
x memos1 9 blocks
x scripts
x scripts/chkfiles 3 blocks
x scripts/doit 1 blocks
```

which indicates that the files were copied from the diskette into the same subdirectories in which they originally were stored.

Thus, you have copied the files and preserved the subdirectory structure that you had in the original directory *lusr/marty*.

You can copy just one file from the diskette into the current directory. To do that you would execute a command like

tar xvf /dev/rfd0 memos1

If you wanted to copy off just one of the files in a subdirectory, you would have to specify the exact name with which it was copied onto the diskette.

The **tar** command can store files in a tar image file on disk rather than on a diskette. Thus, the command

tar cvf marty.tar marty

will store all of the files in the directory *marty* in a file called *marty.tar*. This file will behave just like any other tar file and can be copied, renamed, and can even be itself copied onto another diskette using the **tar** command.

A tar image file on disk can be compressed using the **compress** command, as in

compress marty.tar

which will create a file called *marty.tar.Z* and delete the *marty.tar* file. This new file will be quite a bit smaller than the original file depending on the contents of the original file. The compressed tar file can itself be placed on a diskette with the **tar** command. This new file can be transferred to a new system more efficiently than can the uncompressed version because it is so much smaller. Don't forget this is a binary file even if the original file was an ASCII text file. Once you have moved the compressed tar file to its new system, you can recreate the original files by first uncompressing the file and next using the **tar** command to extract the individual files. The combination of the **tar** and **compress** commands can be used to imitate the functionality of the **pkzip** and **pkunzip** DOS commands.

Finally, if you need to move files between two different UNIX systems, you can use a tar image of the files that you want to transfer. The format of the tar image is more or less standard across UNIX systems.

Exercises

For some of these exercises, place a diskette in the diskette drive that can be written on.

1. Write the contents of your home directory to a diskette using the **tar** command. What command did you use? What files are on the diskette? How do you know?

2. Following the directory structure shown in Figure 3.1, make a tar image of the file *memo1*, files *manual1*, *ord.12* in the subdirectory *docs* and file *helloworld.c* in subdirectory *source*. What command did you use? Is there any other command that you could use? Will the contents of the tar image be different between these two commands?

3. Write the contents of your home directory to a diskette using the **doscp** command if you are on a SCO system or the **doswrite** command if you are on an IBM system. You may need to format the diskette. What command did you use? Take the diskette to a DOS system and make sure that you can read that diskette. What command did you use on the DOS system?

4. Are diskettes on UNIX systems always formatted the same? On DOS systems? Can a diskette formatted on one UNIX system be read on another UNIX system?

13

Networking and Client/Server

OVERVIEW

Suppose that you had a second UNIX system on which you needed to execute a particular application, what would you do? Figure 1.3 illustrated the architecture of a UNIX system and showed just one UNIX system, where all the commands that were executed by that user at that terminal were executed on the UNIX host to which the terminal was attached. You could purchase another terminal and connect that terminal to the second UNIX system, but that would be costly and would clutter up your desk. You want to be able to run an application on that second system from the same terminal that you used to run applications on the original UNIX system. Networking your UNIX systems is what needs to be accomplished.

The first part of this chapter will examine a variety of UNIX networks and introduce the concepts of local area network and wide area network. The next part of the chapter will discuss how client/server networks operate and where UNIX fits into this picture. Finally, a new kind of terminal, the X terminal, will be examined and possible uses will be shown.

WHAT DO UNIX NETWORKS LOOK LIKE?

UNIX systems can be networked in a peer-to-peer arrangement in which each UNIX host is equivalent. Figure 13.1 illustrates two UNIX hosts in a local area network (LAN) with numbers of terminals attached to each. Each networkable UNIX host contains the same components as a standalone host, with the addition of one component—the network interface—which provides the hardware to connect the host to a network. The network can be viewed as a wire to which all the hosts will be connected. This view of a network is oversimplified, but a more detailed view is beyond the scope of this book.

From a very early development stage, network support was built into the UNIX systems. The rules for connecting UNIX hosts to a network in a peer-to-peer mode is called the *Transmission Control Protocol / Internet Protocol*, or more commonly *TCP/IP*. A protocol is a set of rules governing the behavior of two communicating hosts. TCP/IP, which is a suite of protocols, defines the services necessary to interconnect processors and even to interconnect networks. TCP/IP is the most widely used protocol available today. Every UNIX system supports it and most other non-UNIX systems have software available for them that supports TCP/IP. The wide availability of common networking software has led to the growth of large complex networks. From a user's point of view, TCP/IP provides a set of applications ("programs") that enable users to interact with remote processors. Also, TCP/IP provides a way to name hosts so that users do not have to know the address of a host, only its name. Figure 13.1 contains two hosts named "mars" and "jupiter." In a network, both the names and addresses of the hosts must be unique.

In a network with two UNIX hosts, the terminals directly attached to UNIX host "mars" can connect to UNIX host "jupiter" using the **rlogin** or **telnet** commands, which are TCP/IP applications. Both of these commands are more fully described in chapter 14. Once connected to a UNIX host "jupiter," a user at one of these terminals can execute commands on UNIX host "jupiter" as if he or she was directly attached to UNIX host "jupiter." The reverse situation is also true—terminals on UNIX host "jupiter" can use the **rlogin** or **telnet** command to connect to UNIX host 1 and execute commands on that host.

UNIX systems will treat all connections as equivalent, regardless of whether the user is local or remote. Thus, applications can be executed on a UNIX host somewhere in a UNIX network without regard to which terminals and users are directly attached, since any user can connect with any UNIX host in a network and execute commands on that UNIX host.

Figure 13.1 shows the network as a "pipe" with the UNIX

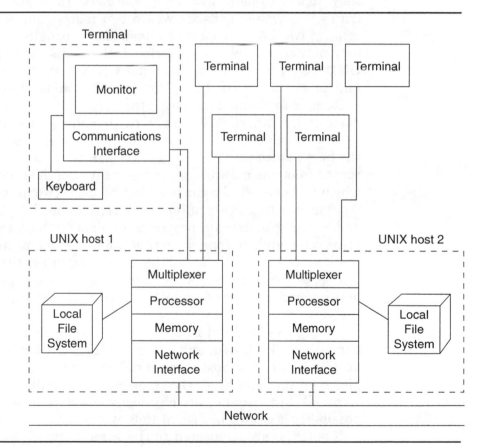

Figure 13.1.   Networked UNIX systems in a local area network.

hosts directly connected. All messages from one UNIX host to another use this pipe. Further, all messages are checked by all hosts attached to this pipe, but only the addressed host will read the message. All UNIX hosts are equivalent in this type of peer-to-peer relationship. This model pictures the UNIX hosts as quite near to each other and the network as one continuous pipe. Networks like this are usually called *local area networks* or *LANs*.

UNIX hosts that are physically located in different buildings or even different cities can be connected together using communications hardware such as routers and bridges, so that logically they appear to be in the same local network. Figure 13.2 illustrates this type of network where two routers and a phone line connect two LANs. This type of network is usually called a wide area network (*WAN*). The principle is the same—terminals on one UNIX host can connect to the other UNIX host and execute commands on that UNIX host. The job of the added hardware, the routers, is to channel messages that are addressed to the UNIX hosts on the other LAN through the telephone line and onto the LAN to which that host is connected. Thus, a message sent from the host named "mars" to a host named "blue" would need to be routed from one network to the other through the telephone line, which is the physical connection between the two networks.

A user sitting at a terminal connected to one of the UNIX hosts and wanting to execute programs on another host executes the same commands to connect to that other host no matter whether the host of interest is in the next room or in another state. Of course, performance may vary depending on the complexity of the network and the type of connection(s) between the various parts of the network.

In Figures 13.1 and 13.2, a terminal is shown as consisting of a monitor, a keyboard, and a communication interface. The connection to the local host is via serial communications to a multiplexer on the local host. These terminals are called "hardwired" terminals because they are physically wired to the host. Another possibility is shown in Figure 13.3, where several personal computers (PCs) are connected to the same network as the UNIX hosts. The networked PC is just like the standalone PC but needs one additional component, a network interface card that performs

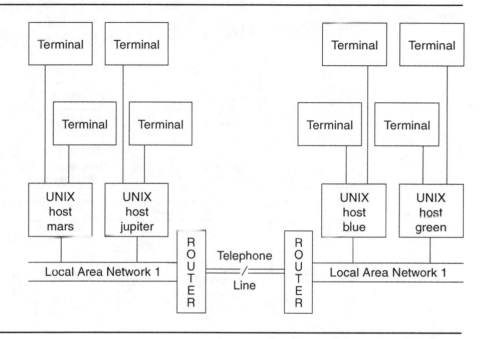

Figure 13.2.   Networked UNIX systems in a wide area network.

the same function for the PC as the network interface component did for the UNIX host. This network interface card connects the PC to the network. Some additional software that provides the TCP/IP capabilities will also need to be installed on the PC.

Once the PC is TCP/IP capable and connected to the network, a program that performs a **telnet** or **rlogin** command is executed on the PC to connect it to the UNIX host of interest. Once connected, no other programs are executed on the PC; all the commands that the user enters on the PC are executed on the UNIX system. The results of these commands are displayed on the PC. This PC implementation of the **telnet** or **rlogin** command will pretend to be a terminal so that the UNIX host will not distinguish between this program and a real terminal. This terminal "pretender" is usually called a *terminal emulator*.

Terminal emulator programs are available from a wide range of companies. Many of these programs can operate in a Windows

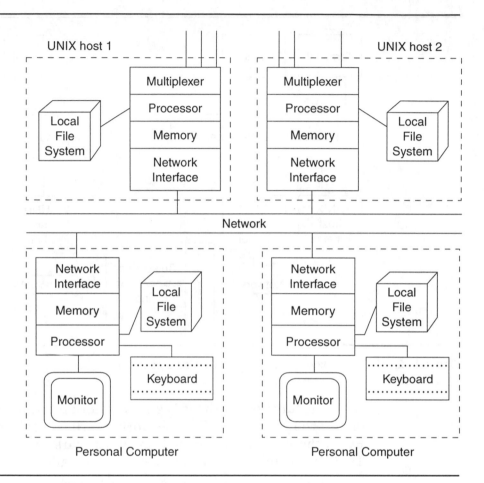

Figure 13.3.   Using personal computers in UNIX networks.

environment on the personal computer. This feature provides the added flexibility of allowing multiple connections to multiple UNIX hosts at the same time. Further, other Windows applications can also be run at the same time. This multiconnection functionality is not available on a hardwired terminal.

These networked PCs can be connected to two networks at the same time through one network interface card, if the networks use different protocols. This functionality will enable a PC to be connected to a UNIX network at the same time it is connected to a Novell network, since the Novell network uses a different protocol suite.

CLIENT/SERVER SYSTEMS

The data traffic that will be incurred by a terminal that is directly connected to one UNIX system while executing on a second UNIX system requires that all of the data displayed on the terminal will be moved through the network. The terminals (even the personal computers that are acting like terminals) do not execute any part of the application; they only display what the application requests them to display. This approach places a heavy burden on the network. Further, the personal computers that are executing a terminal emulator program are using very little of their own resources to display the responses from the UNIX host.

One goal of current networking strategies is to bring important business data to any person within a company who needs that data, no matter how removed from the data that person is. In other words, if a worker in a company needs some data to do his or her job, the location of that data should not be an impediment to providing that data to that worker. Distributing that data to the workers in the company is part of the justification for creating the network. This important data could be provided in files that are moved through the network to the computer to which the worker is attached. If changes were needed to that data, it would have to be moved back to the host that was storing that data after all the changes had been made. Using files to distribute the important data would cause large amounts of data traffic in the network just to move the data to the proper host.

The client/server technology was created to provide access to data on remote hosts while easing the network traffic burden. A sample client/server network is displayed in Figure 13.4, where a UNIX server is interacting with three clients. In a client/server network, the client requests from the server only the data that the client wants to display or operate on. The formatting of the data and the labeling of the fields and any other decorations (graphic images) would be stored and executed on the client. In addition, any calculations on the data that would be needed to display the data in the form that the remote user wants would be

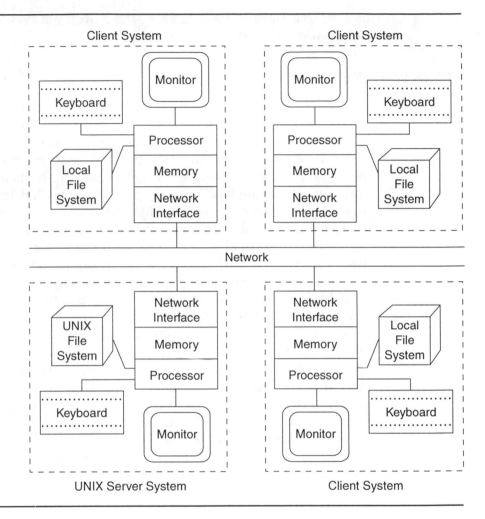

Figure 13.4.   Architectural view of client/server system.

performed on the client. Thus, the network need only carry the individual data elements from the server to the client and vice versa, but does not need to carry any other information. Thus, the server system will only be executing programs that provide data but do little else for the client application. Because of this, the server system can be optimized for only data management.

Figure 13.4 shows that the hardware configuration needed for the client is a personal computer connected via the network to the server. Data is provided by the server to the client through the network. The personal computer will execute the client application software; a local file system on the personal computer is needed to store the software to be executed and any graphics images that are needed as part of the application. No application data will be stored on the client system. After changes have been made to the data by the client, the data will be sent back to the server to be stored and made available to other clients.

Only data is moved between server and client. All operations that are needed to display the data are performed by the client itself, thus minimizing the data traffic in the network.

Figure 13.4 displays a client/server network that uses a UNIX system as a server. Often the data is stored in a database, which is a set of software designed to provide fast, efficient access to the data stored within it. These databases and the systems that provide the data access are optimized to provide data. Instead of a UNIX system, a DOS system could be used as a database server. The hardware configuration would contain much the same elements. UNIX systems as servers are better suited for larger applications where either the number of clients is large or the amount of data to be managed is large. One advantage of client/server software is that the client does not know (or care) what type of system is providing data to it. Thus, a client/server system could be implemented with a smaller server like a DOS system, and a larger server such as a UNIX system could be added later when the demands on the system have increased.

X TERMINALS ON UNIX SYSTEMS

The terminals shown in Figures 13.1, 13.2, and 13.3 are only required to display text. Development of graphically oriented applications began a number of years ago and terminals that could display graphics were needed for these applications. Terminals for UNIX systems that could display graphics images, much like Windows programs on a DOS system, were developed in the last five years. These terminals are called *X terminals*, because the protocol that is used to display the graphics on these terminals is based on a graphics language developed by MIT called "X". This graphics language requires terminals that can process display requests instead of just displaying information.

Data and the instructions on how to display that data ("X commands") are sent from the UNIX host to the X terminal. The X terminal must process these X commands to create the graphics image to display on the terminal. Thus, an X terminal needs its own processor and memory in which to execute the graphics commands that are requested by the application programs executing on the UNIX host. Further, these X terminals need a Network Interface component to connect to the network just like a UNIX host. Figure 13.5 illustrates a network that contains three of these X terminals and a UNIX host on which the graphics application is executing.

The images that are shown on X terminals are displayed in windows that operate like windows on a PC. A window manager application is also executed to manage placement and sizing of windows, much like the Program Manager does in DOS Windows applications.

X terminals, as shown in Figure 13.5, are devices that can only execute X graphics commands. Neither the application data nor the application executables are stored on the X terminal. Further, the programs that are needed to execute X commands also can be downloaded to the X terminal when that terminal starts operating. Thus, as illustrated in Figure 13.5, no file system local to the X terminal is necessary. These X terminals that have no local storage place a heavy burden on the network. For performance reasons, X terminals will often have a small local file system so that programs, fonts (sets of characters to be displayed), and graphic images can be stored on the X terminal and not be repeatedly downloaded from the UNIX host.

DOS programs that can "emulate" an X terminal have been written for the PC. These emulated X terminals, as shown in Figure 13.6, execute a program on a PC that can process the X display commands and display the graphics the same as any real X terminal can. An emulated X terminal has the same components as any other networked PC. These PCs are sent the X display commands to execute through the network just like a real X terminal.

One advantage of an emulated X terminal is that these PCs can execute any of the other PC programs at the same time that they are emulating an X terminal in a window.

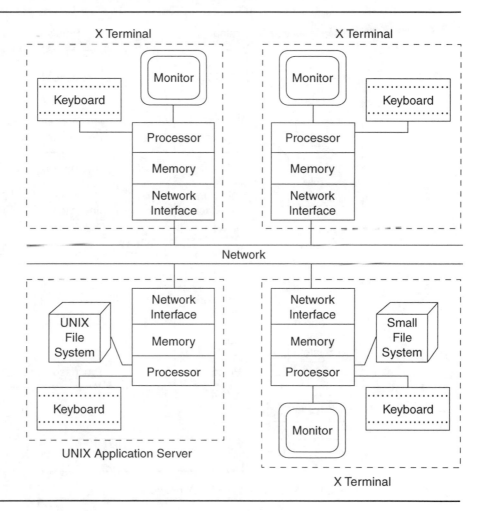

Figure 13.5.   X terminals in a UNIX network.

WHAT KIND OF TERMINAL TO USE ON A UNIX SYSTEM

A number of different kinds of terminals have been described in this chapter—simple hardwired terminals, network-capable PCs, and X terminals. The simpler the capabilities of the terminal, the less expensive it is. For example, a terminal suitable for hardwiring to a UNIX host is available for less than $500. A network-capable PC with software will cost somewhere around $2000. An X termi-

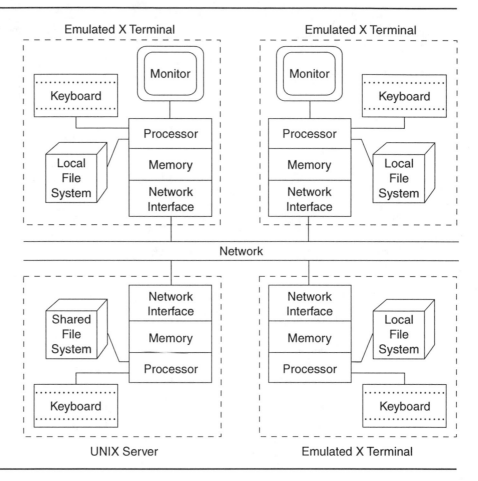

Figure 13.6. "Emulated" X terminals in a UNIX network.

nal runs about $1750 and up as you choose faster processors and more memory. A PC to emulate an X terminal can start at $2000 and go up from there, depending on processor and memory.

Choose the type of terminal that fits the requirements of the applications that you want to run. Clearly the networked PC provides the most flexibility, because with the appropriate software, the networked PC can run any of the various kinds of applications that a UNIX host might want, including terminal emulation, client/server, or X emulation. Obviously, the network connections would need to be built so that the PC could do all of these functions. In recent years many institutions have committed to providing the infrastructure so that all of the "terminals" are really PCs running some kind of emulation or application software.

Exercise

This lab exercise requires that you can access a network of several UNIX systems. The **telnet** command used in this exercise is discussed in detail in the next chapter.

1. Use the **telnet** command to sign onto another system. How can you determine what the name of this new system is? Now **telnet** onto another system or back on the system that you started from. Can the UNIX system determine that you have connected to it from the network? Does the UNIX host care?

Using TCP/IP Commands

OVERVIEW

Chapter 13 described a variety of UNIX networks with each network having several UNIX hosts. The rules that make communications between UNIX hosts effective are called the Transmission Control Protocol / Internet Protocol (TCP/IP). This chapter will discuss how users can interact with remote systems. Users often wish either to use the files of another UNIX system or to run applications on another UNIX system. The users might be physically connected to one UNIX system in a network and the remote UNIX system of interest is somewhere else in the network. This chapter will focus on the TCP/IP commands you would use to establish a user session on a remote UNIX system (the **rlogin** and **telnet** commands), to move files around in a network from one UNIX system to another (the **rcp** and **ftp** commands), and to interact with a remote system without establishing a connection to it (the **rsh** command). Finally, the UNIX version of file sharing between UNIX hosts is discussed.

For DOS-based personal computer systems connected to networks, software can be purchased that implements many of the commands described in this chapter, such as **rlogin**, **telnet**, and **ftp**. This software can enable the user on the personal computer to interact with a UNIX system on a peer-to-peer relationship as illustrated in Figure 13.3.

USING rlogin **COMMAND TO CONNECT TO A REMOTE HOST**

To connect to any UNIX host, you would log into that host as described in chapter 2. To log onto a remote system and begin a terminal system with it, you need to use a special command, the **rlogin** command. Any commands that you execute after you log in on the remote system will be executed on the remote system, just as if you were logged into a local system. The **rlogin** command needs the name of the host to connect to. The **rlogin** command looks like

rlogin host1

which will connect you to the remote host named *host1* and then start the login process on that remote host. The remote host will request your password with the message:

```
password:
```

which is a request for your password on the remote host. You would enter your password. If both user name and password are valid, you would be connected to *host1*. Now any commands that you enter would be executed on *host1*. Your password on a remote system does not have to be the same as your password on the local system.

By default the **rlogin** command assumes that you wish to use the same user name on the remote host as you are using on the local host. If you want instead to login to a remote host under a different name, the **-l** option is available to specify the name of the user under which you want to execute on the remote host. For example,

rlogin host1 -l newusername

will start an interactive terminal session on the remote host named *host1* under the name *newusername*. The interactive session will be started in the home directory of *newusername* and the environment will be what the user *newusername* has set up.

You end a remote session just as you end a local session by

logging out of the remote host, usually with the **exit** command or sometimes with the **logout** command.

USING telnet COMMAND TO CONNECT TO A REMOTE HOST

Another method of connecting to a remote host is to use the **telnet** command. The simplest use of the **telnet** command is to establish an interactive terminal session with a remote host to execute commands on that remote host. To do this, enter the following:

telnet hostname

which will cause the **telnet** command to establish a connection with the remote host named *hostname* and the following will display on your terminal:

```
trying . . . .
Connection to hostname
Escape character is "^T"
```

followed by several blank lines. Then the **telnet** command will start a login session with the host named *hostname*. The **telnet** command does not provide the name of a user, so the remote host will prompt for your login name and then your login password. After both responses have been entered and validated, commands are executed on that remote host from then on until the **logout** command is entered or the telnet session is halted.

In its simplest form the **telnet** command does exactly the same function as the **rlogin** command. But **telnet** provides several additional functions that **rlogin** command does not. The **telnet** provides the **-8** option, which will force an eight-bit data path to be used for the connection from the local host to the remote host. Another important feature is the ability to choose to which TCP port on the remote host you wish to be connected to. With this functionality, you can connect to the mail server on a remote host or configure a terminal server remotely.

USING rcp COMMAND TO COPY FILES FROM HOST TO HOST

Copying files from one UNIX host to another UNIX host can be accomplished using the **rcp** command, provided that you have valid user names on both systems. In order to perform the simplest of **rcp** commands, to copy a file from one host to another, you would use the syntax:

>**rcp file1 host1:file2**

which will copy the contents of *file1* that is on the local host to the remote host *host1* and call it *file2*. If, alternatively, *file1* is on a remote host (*host1*) and you wish to copy it to your local host and call it *file2*, you would use:

>**rcp host1:file1 file2**

If the name of the file on the local host will be the same as the name of the file on the remote host, the specification of the name on the local host can be replaced with a period (.). Thus,

>**rcp host1:file1 .**

will copy *file1* from the remote host *host1* to the local host as *file1*. If the file you want to copy is not on the local host but on a remote host (*host1*) and you want to copy it to a remote host (*host2*), you would use:

>**rcp host1:file1 host2:file2**

which would copy *file1* on *host1* to *file2* on *host2*.

If the name of a directory is used as the destination instead of the name of a file, then the source file is copied into the destination directory and keeps its original name. Thus,

>**rcp file1 host2:directory2**

indicates that *file1* will be copied to *directory2* on *host2*. Also, it is possible to list several files that are to be copied into the directory, for example, as in the following command:

>**rcp file1 file2 file3 host2:directory2**

which will cause *file1*, *file2*, and *file3* all to be copied into *directory2* on host *host2*. If the path of the destination file or directory is not fully qualified (that is to say, does not begin with a "/"), the path is interpreted as beginning at the home directory of the remote user account, which will be the same as the local user account unless otherwise specified.

USING ftp COMMAND TO TRANSFER FILES BETWEEN HOSTS

Another method of transferring files between hosts, which has no network limitations or any system dependencies, is called **ftp**, file transfer program. **ftp** is a command-driven general purpose file transfer program that can transfer files between systems of differing architectures, providing they both support TCP/IP protocol. In addition, the **ftp** command has an extensive set of commands to allow you to create a script to drive the copying process. If you just issue the **ftp** command by itself, as in:

ftp

the reply will be:

```
ftp>
```

If you need assistance remembering what commands are available, you can enter **help** or **?** and you will have displayed on your terminal:

```
Commands may be abbreviated. Commands are:
!          delete     mdelete  proxy       runique
$          debug      mdir     sendport    send
account    dir        mget     put         size
append     disconnect mkdir    pwd         status
ascii      form       mls      quit        struct
bell       get        mode     quote       sunique
binary     glob       modtime  recv        system
bye        hash       mput     remotehelp  tenex
case       help       nmap     rstatus     trace
cd         image      nlist    rhelp       type
cdup       lcd        ntrans   rename      user
close      ls         open     reset       verbose
cr         macdef     prompt   rmdir       ?
```

and then an ftp prompt would again be displayed. The next command you would normally enter is **open host1** to connect to *host1*. After you entered your user id and password, you would be ready to do file operations. You are now connected to another host solely for the purpose of performing file operations. You will not be able to execute any commands that are not associated with files, and you will not be able to execute application programs.

If you wanted to specify the name of the host to connect to on the command line, you would give the command:

ftp goofy

which would attempt to connect to the host named *goofy*. If the connection is successful, a message such as:

```
Connected to goofy.
```

will appear. The ftp server on the remote host will usually send back a set of opening messages such as:

```
220 goofy FTP server (Version wu-2.4(1)
                Mon Jul 18 11:53:55 CDT 1994)
```

Finally, the ftp server on that host will ask for your name with the message:

```
Name (goofy:marty):
```

to which the user would answer with his name. If you are a defined user of this system you would enter the user name by which you are known on that system. For a login as a guest, you would answer: *anonymous*. See a later section in this chapter for a discussion of what facilities ftp provides for public access to a system. The remote ftp server would then prompt you for a password with the messages:

```
331 Guest login ok, send your complete
e-mail address as password.
```

```
Password:
```

You would then reply with the appropriate password, which for public access would be *marick@mycompany.com*, which is a complete e-mail address. If this login sequence is accepted, the remote ftp server would give the message:

```
230 Guest login ok, access restrictions apply.
```

Now the user is ready to transfer files. First, the user might want to change to a directory where the files of interest are and ask for a list of the files in that directory as in:

cd source
ls

to which the ftp server would reply with a list of files:

```
200 PORT command successful.
150 Opening ASCII mode data connection for
file list.
applsource
program1.c.old
program1.c
program2.c
program3.c
226 Transfer complete.
```

and then the local ftp client would again display the ftp prompt *ftp>*. If the user wanted to transfer the file *program1.c*, he or she would enter the command

get program1.c

and the replies would be:

```
200 PORT command successful.
150 Opening ASCII mode data connection for
        program1.c (567 bytes).
226 Transfer complete.
578 bytes received in 0.2343 seconds (2.409
Kbytes/s)
```

and the ftp prompt would be displayed, indicating that another command could be entered. Figure 14.1 is the dialogue that would be displayed if the user wanted to transfer two files *appl1.c* and *appl2.c* from the *applsource* directory. After the user has transferred the files of interest and wants to end the session, he or she would enter the command **quit** and the connection would be ended. A summary of the most useful **ftp** commands is shown in Table 14.1. The **ftp** command **get** is used to retrieve files and **put**

```
ftp> cd applsource
250 CWD command successful.
ftp> get appl1.c
200 PORT command successful.
150 Opening ASCII mode data connect for appl1.c (5867
bytes).
226 Transfer complete.
5996 bytes received in 0.1843 seconds (31.78 Kbytes/s)
ftp> ls *index*.*
200 PORT command successful.
150 Opening ASCII mode data connection for file list.
 appl1.c
 appl2.c
 appl3.c
 test.c
226 Transfer complete.
ftp> get appl2.c
200 PORT command successful.
150 Opening ASCII mode data connect for appl2.c (3859
bytes).
226 Transfer complete.
173092 bytes received in 7.725 seconds (21.88 Kbytes/s)
ftp>
```

Figure 14.1.   Dialogue during an **ftp** transfer of two files.

is used to deliver files to the remote system. You can request the retrieval of several files by using the **mget** command, as in

> **mget appl***

which would request the transfer of all files that start with *appl*. **ftp** will ask your permission before transferring a file

```
mget appl1.c?
```

to which you would reply "y" if you wish to transfer the file or "n" if you do not. Then **ftp** will ask about the next file that you requested. In this way you can request the transfer of a group of files and pick out the one file that you actually want to transfer.

Table 14.1.   Important **ftp** Commands

ftp Command	What it does
binary	Sets the file transfer type to binary image.
cd rdir	Changes the working directory on the remote host to the *rdir* directory.
get rfile [lfile]	Copies the remote file *rfile* to the local host. If *lfile* is not specified, the remote file name is used locally.
lcd ldir	Changes the working directory on the local host.
mget rfiles	Expands *rfiles* at the remote host and copies the indicated remote files to the current directory on the local host.
mkdir rdir	Creates the directory *rdir* on the remote host.
mput lfiles	Expands local files at the local host and copies the indicated local files to the remote host.
open host	Establishes a connection to the ftp server at the specified *host*.
put lfile [rfile]	Stores a local file *lfile* on the remote host as the *rfile* file if specified.
pwd	Displays the name of the current directory on the remote host.
quit	Closes the connection and exits command.
user uname [password]	Identifies the local user as *uname* to the remote FTP server. If *password* is not specified and the remote server requires it, the **ftp** command prompts for it locally.

USING rsh COMMANDS TO EXECUTE COMMANDS ON A REMOTE HOST

Suppose you only wanted some information about the remote system, for example, what date and time the remote system was set for. You did not want to execute an interactive command; you just wanted to ask the system for the information. Single commands can be executed on a remote host using the **rsh** command, as in

    rsh host1 commandname

which will execute the command **commandname** on the remote host called *host1*. For example, the command:

    rsh host1 df

will request the amount of available free disk space on remote host *host1*.

    Almost any command can be executed on the remote host. If the command is not allowed because the user does not have the privilege to execute the command, the command will be rejected by the remote host. The rsh server executes the requested command under the user id of the user on the local host who requested the command. The commands are executed on the remote host using the *HOME* directory of the user (as defined in the */etc/passwd* file on the remote host). Thus, files that do not have an absolute path specified for them will be searched for in the *HOME* directory of the user on the remote host. For example,

    rsh host1 cp file1 file2

will look for *file1* in the *HOME* directory of the user on the remote host and will copy its contents to *file2* in the *HOME* directory on the remote host *host1*.

    To execute a command under a different user name, use the "-l" (letter L) option on the command line following the name of the remote host. The following command will execute the **cat /etc/passwd** command under the user id *tom*:

    rsh host1 -l tom cat /etc/passwd

A different user id might be needed if the local user does not have the necessary level of privilege on the remote host or is not even known on the remote host.

USING mount COMMAND TO ACCESS REMOTE FILES

Network file services can be invoked by the user by executing the **mount** command, which requests that file systems on a remote host be made available on the local host for users to access locally. These file systems may be local (actually physically attached to the local host) or they may be remote (that is to say, physically attached to a remote host). The **mount** comma quires that the user know which is the case, but once the **m** command is successful, this distinction will not be visible. **mount** command is:

mount remotehost:/goodstuff /goodstuff

which is a request to mount a directory on *remotehost* called */goodstuff* as */goodstuff* on the local system. A remote file system can be mounted on a local system under a name that is different from its name on the remote system. Users can be confused by this because when they are logged into the remote system, they will see a different name for the same files. Thus, remote file systems are often mounted on a local system using the identical name as the remote file system. Once a file system is successfully mounted, changing to the */goodstuff* directory on the local system will make available to the local user the same files that a user on the remote system sees.

A user can determine if a file is on the local host or on the remote host by using the **df** command or by examining the permissions attributes of the file. The **df** command is simply

df /happy/large

which requests information about the directory */happy/large* and the information may look like:

```
Filesystem    Total KB  used    free   %used  Mounted on
happy:/large  1247180 1077308 169872  86%    /happy/large
```

which indicates that the directory */happy/large* is actually on a remote host named *happy*. Often remote file systems are named using the name of the remote host as the top-level directory name, but this is not required. If the user executes the command

ls -l /happy

the display would be

```
Drwxrwxrwx 32 root    adm    1024 Sep 17 18:01 large/
```

For the command

ls -l /happy/large

the display would be

```
Frw-r-----  1 marty   adm    7600 Sep 10 15:26 acaca.prtx
Drwxr-xr-x  2 marty   adm     512 Jul 07 16:02 about/
Frwxr-xr-x  1 marty   adm    9922 Aug 31 16:50 backup.out*
Drwxr-xr-x  2 marty   adm     512 Aug 18 17:31 config/
Drwxr-xr-x  2 marty   adm     512 Jul 09 16:12 convert/
Frwxr-xr-x  2 marty   adm    4434 Sep 11 16:12 commit*
Frw-r-----  1 marty   adm   13927 Aug 31 14:21 database
```

where the capital letters *F* to designate a file and *D* to designate
a directory indicate these are remotely located files and directories. Unfortunately, not every version of UNIX marks remote
files this way; some versions do not change the permissions on a
remote file.

To obtain a list of the file systems available on a host, the user
would use the **df** command. As an example, a display of the various file systems on a particular host is presented in Figure 14.2.
For this system there were two file systems from the host *jerico*
plus one system each from the hosts *happy*, *goofy* and *sleepy*. The
file systems called */dev/hdX* are local file systems. Note that it is
not necessary that the directory name on the remote host be the
same as the directory name on the local host. For practical reasons, system administrators generally include the name of the
remote host in the name by which the local host knows that file
system.

Filesystem	Total KB	used	free	%used	Mounted on
/dev/hd4	53248	42388	10860	79%	/
/dev/hd2	253952	249224	4728	98%	/usr
/dev/hd9var	4096	1980	2116	48%	/var
/dev/hd3	8192	1188	7004	14%	/tmp
jerico:/usr/local	262144	232752	29392	88%	/usr/local
jerico:/u	49152	44280	4872	90%	/u
happy:/large	1247180	1077308	169872	86%	/happy/large
goofy:/usr/local2	81548	63572	17976	77%	/usr/local2
sleepy:/good	524280	33744	490536	6%	/good

Figure 14.2.   Sample output from **df** command.

Exercises

1. Connect to a UNIX system. Create a file called *goodfile*. Now connect to another UNIX system from your local UNIX host. How did you do that? If you used the **telnet** command, why didn't you use **rlogin** command? If you used the **rlogin** command, why didn't you use **telnet** command? Copy the file *goodfile* from one UNIX host to another. Describe two different methods to accomplish this. What commands did you use?

2. If you have access to the Internet connect to the archive server: *wuarchive.wustl.edu*. You may have to attempt this at an off-hour because this server is very busy. Now retrieve the file *part01.Z* from the directory *usenet/comp.sources.unix/volume27/encode*. What commands did you use?

3. Create a shell script to retrieve a file from an Internet host and pass in three arguments to the script: (1) name of host, (2) name of directory, and (3) name of file to retrieve. Make sure that you create a log file. While you are connected to the Internet host, get a list of the directory so that you can determine why the retrieval process fails (if it does).

4. What method would you use if you wanted to copy a file from a remote system to your local system but were not known to that remote system? Are there any choices?

5. Display the file systems on your local UNIX host. Are there any which are not physically on this local UNIX host? How do you know? Is it possible to make the files on any UNIX host available locally on the UNIX host?

Introduction to the Internet

OVERVIEW

As discussed in earlier chapters, TCP/IP is found on all UNIX hosts and many non-UNIX hosts as well. The wide availability of a common standard communications protocol led to the establishment of institution-wide networks using TCP/IP to provide easy access to information within a company. Since many institutional networks were using a common protocol, exchanging information *between institutions* became possible and a network that allowed communications between institutions could be created. Thus, the Internet was born.

The first part of this chapter discusses what the Internet is and what services are offered on the Internet. Succeeding sections examine each of the four basic Internet functions—electronic mail, Usenet newsgroups, file transfer between computers, and remote login to another computer, in detail. Finally Internet browsers are discussed.

WHAT IS THE INTERNET?

The Internet is a worldwide network of computer networks communicating with each other using the TCP/IP protocol. Every network site on the Internet has a unique name and address assigned by an Internet organizing body called the Merit Network Information Center, which coordinates the assignment of unique names and addresses. The Internet can be viewed as one large network where the distinguishable parts are the systems whose names are known and the rest of the network is just there to provide connectivity to the systems of interest. Figure 15.1 illustrates that view by showing all of the Internet as a "cloud" of computer systems with the known target systems themselves connected to this cloud. In Figure 15.1 the local site is *goofy.mycmpny.com* and the remote sites (actual Internet site names) are *wuarchive.wustl.edu*, *gatekeeper.dec.com*, and *town.hall.org*.

Names of systems in the Internet usually have from two to four levels as shown in Figure 15.1, each separated by a period (.). Single level names such as "mars" or "jupiter" would not be unique enough for a large network. The lowest level usually identifies what kind of a site it is or what foreign country it is in. For example, a company's Internet name will end in *.com*, a government institution in *.gov*, an educational institution in *.edu*, an organization in *.org*, an Australian site in *.au*, an English site in *.uk*, and so on. Thus, in Figure 15.1, *wuarchive.wustl.edu* is a university (Washington University in St. Louis), *gatekeeper.dec.com* is a company (Digital Equipment Corporation), and *town.hall.org*

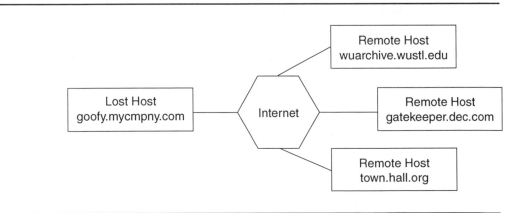

Figure 15.1.   One view of the Internet.

is an organization. One famous government Internet site is *whitehouse.gov*.

Certain sites are designated as routing sites so that messages can be sent through the network from one site to another, even if these two sites are not in the same network. Information about where in the network individual sites are located is sent around the Internet to all of the routing sites so that when a message for a particular site arrives at a routing site, that site will know where next to send the message.

The Internet provides four services to its users: electronic mail, Usenet newsgroups, file transfer between computers, and remote login to another computer. In order to use any of these services (except for electronic mail) you must first be logged into a local host that has access to the Internet. Each of these services can be invoked from the command line using a serial connection. Thus, even using modems and a phone line as a serial connection to log into a host that has access to the Internet enables all of these functions. This type of account is sometimes called a "shell" account because you are operating under the control of a shell program as discussed in chapter 2. Some newer Internet browsing software that provides a graphical view of the Internet and has menus of functions and automates the searching of Internet sites for information and the transfer of files requires a network connection to the Internet. Usually this is done with a Network Interface board as discussed in chapter 13, but special dial-up connections can provide a network connection using modems; these connections are called Serial Line Interface Protocol (SLIP) connections. How these operate is beyond the scope of this book.

SENDING A MESSAGE TO SOMEONE ON THE INTERNET

Sending mail to another user on your system or within your network was discussed in chapter 11. For that case the command that was invoked looked like

mail fred

and the network looked like the ones shown in chapter 13. But suppose you wanted to send mail to someone who was not on your system and is not even registered as a user of your system. As an example, suppose you wanted to send mail to the user *fred* who is known to the system *remote.system.com* that is connected to the Internet as illustrated in Figure 15.1. The **mail** command will handle this operation for you if you know the name of a system on which that user is known. To aid the **mail** command, you must add the name of the system to the name of the user as in

> **mail fred@remote.system.com**

which would send the message to the system *remote.system.com* to be delivered to the user *fred*. Once you enter this command, the **mail** command will operate just as described in chapter 11. As described earlier, the mail will be delivered, even if the user is not currently on the system. The **mail** command does not care to whom you are sending the message. Furthermore, if you address your message incorrectly, the **mail** command will send it anyway. If the message proves to be undeliverable, you will receive a message that will inform you of the failure.

For your message to be delivered to the intended user, some intermediate hosts will need to route your message from your system to the *remote.system.com* system. The routing sites in the Internet know about the systems that are connected to the Internet, and thus can figure out how to send your message to that site.

The mail protocol services that the Internet provides are much the same as the mail services that are available in your own computer network. You even construct the message in the same way. The only difference is that the person to whom the message is addressed is located somewhere in the Internet and not in your local computer network. When someone that is not on your system sends you a message, you can use the same **mail** program to read that message.

The name of the system that you specify must be the name that has been registered with the Internet organization and known to other hosts in the Internet. The system's name within the local network may be different. Once the message has been delivered to the named system, the address can be changed to an internal address that might not be known to the systems on the Internet. Thus, in Figure 15.1 the system that is known as *goofy.mycmpny.com* to the Internet may be known as just *goofy* within the local network.

READING USENET NEWSGROUPS ON THE INTERNET

Part of the function of the Internet is for users to exchange information. Two users sending mail to each other are exchanging messages, but only the two users that exchanged the messages will get to read them. More information could be exchanged if there was some way people could send messages that would be distributed to many Internet sites. The Internet society solved this problem by creating a conferencing system that organizes the information around a set of "newsgroups" that cover a very wide range of topics of interest.

Reading the newsgroups is quite simple; just execute one of the news reader commands as in

trn

and you will receive a response like

```
Unread news in ne.food            23 articles
Unread news in ne.forsale        121 articles
Unread news in comp.archives       4 articles
Unread news in comp.dcom.servers  29 articles
Unread news in comp.misc         113 articles
```

```
etc.
======  23 unread articles in ne.food -- read now? [+ynq]
```

The news reader keeps a list of which newsgroups each user is interested in and summarizes what "articles" you have not read in each newsgroup. An article is a message that someone has sent to this newsgroup. An extensive set of help messages will lead you through the techniques of reading newsgroups and subscribing to newsgroups. You can choose to read a newsgroup or skip that group until later.

You inform the Internet of your interest in newsgroups by "subscribing" to that newsgroup and reading the messages that others have sent to that newsgroup. Newsgroups covering any computer topic are available. This type of conferencing is similar to sending messages to mailing lists of users who have expressed interest in some set of ideas.

Once you choose to read a newsgroup, you will be provided with a list of the articles that you have not read and their titles as in

```
      comp.dcom.servers        28 articles

   a  Robert Mah            2  Experiences using LANs...
      shai@pixel.co.il
   b  Brian J. Smith        1  >Terminal servers ...
   d  mick@woodstock.g      1  >Best Server/router?
   e  Me@telematrix.co      3  New Telecom Resource...
      Leonard Conn
      C Hollenbaugh
   f  Barbara Gavin         1  Client\Server Seminars:...
   g  Steve Morytko         2  Authentication for ...
      Carl Rigney
   i  Brad                  2  Vendors FAQ
      Wolfgang Henke
   j  Alwin Mulder          1  On Demand servers
   l  Rudi van Drunen       1  Annex routing
   o  Benjamin BROCHET      1  Avis a tous les ...
   r  Bill Neal             1  Slipping on Citrix?
   s  James Taylor          2  Net Access With TV ...
      John Holmes
   t  Elazar                1  Where can I find DEC's...

   -- Select threads (date order) -- Top 67% [>Z] --
```

where the author of the article is shown at the left and the title of the article is shown at the right. The news reader organizes the messages into "threads," which are messages that relate to each other. The number of the messages in any thread is the number shown between the author and the title. You can choose any of these threads to read by pressing the letter at the far left for the messages of interest or skip to the next page of messages by pressing the spacebar on your terminal.

Newsgroups cover many different interests from a wide range of computer topics to music to art to food, and so on. New newsgroups can be easily formed when new topics of interest are discovered. A few of the newsgroups to which you might subscribe are listed in Table 15.1. This table is just a very small selection of the newsgroups, which number in the thousands.

When users want to contribute their ideas about a topic of interest, they send a message, not to a particular user, but to the newsgroup that has that topic as its focus. This operation is called "posting news" and uses a command called **Pnews**. Once a message has been posted to the newsgroup, everyone who reads that

Table 15.1.   Some Usenet Newsgroups Available on the Internet

Newsgroup	Discussion Topic
comp.archives	Software available via Anonymous ftp
comp.unix.aix	General IBM AIX
comp.unix.hp	General HP Unix
comp.unix.questions	General UNIX questions
comp.unix.shell	UNIX shell programming
comp.unix.wizards	UNIX internals, system administration
comp.answers	Answers to Frequently Asked Questions (FAQ)
comp.dcom.servers	Data communications servers TCP/IP discussions
news.announce.conferences	Announcement of conferences
news.announce.conferences	Announcement of conferences
news.announce.newsgroups	Announcement of new newsgroups
comp.org.ieee	IEEE discussions
rec.music	General music interests
comp.music	Computer music
ne.food	Restaurants in New England
ne.forsale	Items for sale in New England

newsgroup will receive that message. Anyone can post a message or a question to a newsgroup; there are no needed qualifications to contribute to any particular newsgroup.

Many newsgroups gather the answers to the most frequently asked questions in a document known as the FAQ (Frequently Asked Questions) list, which is posted to the newsgroup on a monthly basis. One archive site, *rtfm.mit.edu*, serves as a repository site for these documents.

Messages from the various newsgroups of interest are gathered by one of your local computer systems by accessing a network news server and downloading messages of interest. An individual user informs his or her own news server about the newsgroups he or she is interested in and the local news server will interrogate the remote news server for the list of new messages and new groups. Only messages that the user wants to read are actually downloaded to the news reader's system.

RETRIEVING INFORMATION FROM THE INTERNET

Another Internet service provides the ability to transfer files between two sites on the Internet. The use of the **ftp** command to transfer files between dissimilar sites within a local network was discussed in chapter 14. This same command can be used to transfer files between your host and an Internet host.

Using the **ftp** command to transfer files requires the user to be known to the system. Thus, for a user to have access to a host, that user has to be defined on that system and a password set up for that user on that system. But suppose a group of people want to make a set of files available to the computing public on a particular host in their facility? If they had to define every user and provide a password for every user, they would not be very willing. Instead the **ftp** command provides a special user id called *anonymous*, which will accept any password and thus provide access by every user to all files that are in the home directory of the *anonymous* user. To make files available to any user that uses this method to connect to your system, you would put those files into that directory (or in a subdirectory in that directory) and give the world "read" permission for those files. This particular functionality of the **ftp** command is used by the Internet sites to make software available to users around the world. Sites that provide this availability are called "archive" sites.

An example of an interactive **ftp** session using the *anonymous* user id is shown in Figure 15.2, where a connection has been made to the archive site named *wuarchive.wustl.edu* to retrieve some software. Following the naming conventions of the Internet, this Internet site is at a university and is, in fact, at Washington University in St. Louis. As a courtesy, you use your Internet electronic mail address as the password so that the archive site can know the name of the users of their Internet site. While connected as the *anonymous* user, all of the directories and files in the home directory of the *anonymous* user are available to retrieve files from or to put files into.

In this particular session, while connected to *wuarchive.wustl.edu*, the directories in the home directory of the *anonymous* user were listed using the **ls** command. Then the working directory was changed to one that contains the files of interest with the command

```
goofy:/usr/marty/save[6]% ftp wuarchive.wustl.edu
Connected to wuarchive.wustl.edu.
220 wuarchive.wustl.edu FTP server (Version wu-2.4(1) Mon Jul 8
11:53:55 CDT 1994) ready.

Name (wuarchive.wustl.edu:marty): anonymous
331 Guest login ok, send your complete e-mail address as password.

Password: marick@mycompany.com (Not displayed)
230- If your FTP client crashes or hangs shortly after login
       (Some messages deleted)
230 Guest login ok, access restrictions apply.

ftp> ls -C
200 PORT command successful.
150 Opening ASCII mode data connection for /bin/ls.
README      decus       graphics    mirrors     pub
README.NFS  doc         index.html  multimedia  systems
bin         edu         info        packages    usenet
core        etc         languages   private
226 Transfer complete.

ftp> cd usenet
250 CWD command successful.

ftp> cd comp.binaries.ibm.pc
250 CWD command successful.

ftp> ls -C
200 PORT command successful.
150 Opening ASCII mode data connection for /bin/ls.
Index volume03 volume07 volume11 volume15 volume19 volume23
volume00 volume04 volume08 volume12 volume16 volume20 volume24
volume01 volume05 volume09 volume13 volume17 volume21 volume25
volume02 volume06 volume10 volume14 volume18 volume22 volume26
226 Transfer complete.

ftp> get Index Index.comp.binaries.ibm.pc
200 PORT command successful.
150 Opening ASCII mode data connection for Index (31556 bytes).
226 Transfer complete.
31872 bytes received in 4.063 seconds (7.661 Kbytes/s)

ftp> quit
221 Goodbye.
```

Figure 15.2.   Connecting as *anonymous* for file transfers.

cd comp.binaries.ibm.pc

Finally, a text listing of all the software in this archive was retrieved with the command:

get Index Index.comp.binaries.ibm.pc

which will transfer the *Index* file to the local system and name that file *Index.comp.binaries.ibm.pc*. After retrieving the listing of the contents of this archive site, we ended the **ftp** session. In general, archive sites maintain a file such as *INDEX*, *index*, or *readme.txt* that describes what the various files are that they are storing in this directory.

While the ftp server provides the ability of a user to access this host using *anonymous* as its user id, the local system administrator must set up the directories and files of *ftp*'s *HOME* directory to have the appropriate permissions.

```
#!/bin/csh -f
#
#    Parameter is number of RFC to retrieve
#
#   (Use of $$ described in C shell Chapter)
echo "" >> /tmp/$$M
#   Send user name and password
echo "user anonymous marick@mycompany.com"
                                  >> /tmp/$$M
# Get into directory of interest
echo "cd internet/documents/fyi" >> /tmp/$$M
echo "get INDEX.fyi" >> /tmp/$$M
echo "cd ../rfc" >> /tmp/$$M
echo "get INDEX.rfc" >> /tmp/$$M
while ( $#argv > 0 )
    echo "get rfc$1.txt" >> /tmp/$$M
    shift
end
echo "quit" >> /tmp/$$M
ftp -nv nis.nsf.net < /tmp/$$M >& ftp.out
sleep 10
rm /tmp/$$M
#
```

Figure 15.3.   C shell script to transfer files.

You can build scripts of **ftp** commands to transfer files without user intervention. You would turn off automatically logging in with a command line argument and provide the name of the user and the password in the set of commands that are read in by the **ftp** command. Figure 15.3 is an example of a C shell script to transfer two files (*INDEX.fyi* and *INDEX.rfc*) and a particular document (*rfcNN.txt*), if NN is specified on the command line. For example, if the command that is entered on the command line is:

ftp_comm 1349

the output that is generated is shown in Figure 15.4, which shows the user *anonymous* with password *guest* logging in on the host *nis.nsf.net* and then retrieving three files, *INDEX.fyi*, *INDEX.rfc*, and *rfc1349.txt*.

A few of the better known archive sites are listed in Table 15.2.

Table 15.2.   Some Popular Archive Sites

Archive Site	Contents
rtfm.mit.edu	Usenet Frequently Asked Questions (FAQ) documents
aixpdslib.seas.ucla.edu	Public RS/6000 AIX Software
oak.oakland.edu wuarchive.wustl.edu	Public software for a wide range of operating systems
ftp.uu.net	Usenet FAQ documents Internet background documents
whitehouse.gov	Presidential position papers, press releases
gatekeeper.dec.com	Recipes from various Usenet groups Public X11 Software
town.hall.org	Filings with the Securities and Exchange Commission
ftp.psi.com	Internet documents, TCP/IP standards documents
mrcnext.cso.uiuc.edu	Full text of a variety of books (known as Project Gutenberg)
cs.uwp.edu	Information on classical music with a guide to CDs
ftp.ncsa.uiuc.edu	Public domain Mosaic
software.watson.ibm.com	IBM Watson Publications
ftp.microsoft.com	Microsoft public software and information

```
Connected to nis.nsf.net.
220 nic.merit.edu FTP server ... 14:33:38 EDT 1994) ready.
331 Guest login ok, send your email address as password.
230- Guest login ok, access restrictions apply.
230- Local time is: Sun Jan 15 10:53:26 1995
250 CWD command successful.
200 PORT command successful.
150 Opening ASCII mode data ... for INDEX.fyi (5422 bytes).
226 Transfer complete.
5565 bytes received in 0.709 seconds (7.665 Kbytes/s)
250 CWD command successful.
200 PORT command successful.
150 Opening ASCII mode ... for INDEX.rfc (290145 bytes).
226 Transfer complete.
296310 bytes received in 13.76 seconds (21.02 Kbytes/s)
200 PORT command successful.
150 Opening ASCII mode ... for rfc1349.txt (68949 bytes).
226 Transfer complete.
70573 bytes received in 3.292 seconds (20.93 Kbytes/s)
221 Goodbye.
```

Figure 15.4.   Output created from tile transfer using C shell script.

LOGGING INTO A COMPUTER ON THE INTERNET

The Internet provides the ability to log into a computer that is at another site anywhere on the Internet using the **telnet** command. This type of access requires only that the user have an account on the remote host, but not on any of the intermediate hosts that are carrying messages between you and the remote computer. The **telnet** command operates just the same whether the computer you are communicating with is in the next room or across the country. Chapter 14 described the **telnet** command in some detail.

Systems that can be accessed through the Internet provide a range of services, from libraries that place their catalogs online, such as the Library of Congress (*locis.loc.gov*), to financial services, such as the Dow Jones News Service. Some of these systems charge for their services. When you access one of these systems, you enter a user name and password so that the charges for online time can be billed to you.

USING AN INTERNET BROWSER

All of the services previously described can be used from the command line but do not provide a user-friendly interface. Once connected to a remote site using **ftp**, neither a menu of available files nor a guide to what information is stored there is presented to the user. To remedy this user interface problem, Internet browsers, which have a graphical face and provide menus of functions and items to choose from, were developed. One of the earliest of these browsers is called Mosaic and is publicly available from *ftp.ncsa.uiuc.edu*. An Internet browser requires a TCP/IP connection to the Internet.

The Internet browser takes advantage of a special kind of Internet server called a World Wide Web (WWW) server. WWW servers provide search functions through the use of hypertext. WWW servers have special addresses called uniform resource locators (URL). To examine the contents of a WWW server, you start your Internet browser and inform your browser of the URL of the WWW server of interest. The browser then queries the server and retrieves a list of resources that are available at that server or that the server knows about. This information is presented to the user as documents with keywords that can be chosen to retrieve new information. A few WWW servers to look at are listed in Table 15.3.

Table 15.3.   Some World Wide Web Sites

WWW Server	WWW Server Contents
http://www.census.gov	Census bureau
http:..www.whitehouse.gov	White House documents to browse
http://sunsite.unc.edu	FAQ browser
http://www.tig.com/IBC/index.html	Internet business
http://www.eren.doe.gov	Department of Energy
http://www.ksc.nasa.gov	Kennedy Space Center
http://www.uniforum.org	Uniforum '95
http://icweb.loc.gov/homepage/ichp.htm	Library of Congress
httpL//cad.ucla.edu/repository/usefule.tarot.html	Tarot card reading

Exercises

1. If you have access to the Internet, connect to the archive server: *wuarchive.wustl.edu*. You may have to attempt this at an off-hour because this server is very busy. Now retrieve the file *part01.Z* from the directory *usenet/comp.sources.unix/volume27/encode*. What commands did you use?

2. Create a shell script to retrieve a file from an Internet host and pass in three arguments to the script: (1) name of host, (2) name of directory, and (3) name of file to retrieve. Make sure that you create a log file. While you are connected to the Internet host, get a list of the directory so that you can determine why the retrieval process fails (if it does).

Answers to Exercises

CHAPTER 2

1. You may not have used any command at all. You may have just sat down in front of a terminal and pressed the **Enter** key. The system will then prompt you.

2. You may not know how to do this at this point in the book. There are several ways to determine this: One way is to look at the prompt character that you are shown. A second way is to display the environment variables, just like you would do in a DOS system.

3. This is just: **date**.

4. The error message you probably got was "command not found." The system does not know what the names of commands are. There is no list of available commands on a UNIX system.

5. You should have used the command: **man date**.

6. How did you do that? Did you find other options for the **who** command that are not discussed in this book? Are you surprised?

7. You use the command **who** to determine who is logged on. Yes, you can be logged onto the system more than once. The system does not count the number of times one user is logged into a system. You had better be shown on the list of logged in users.

8. You would use the command: **who am i** to determine who the system thinks you are. You used the **who** command to display cpu time taken by each user.

9. You would use the command: **w**. Users that have been idle for a long time must be sleeping at their terminal. Or they just forgot to end their session and the system doesn't force you to log out.

10. You would use the command: **passwd**.

11. You would use the command: **logout** or **exit**, depending on the shell you were running under.

12. A record is kept of the commands that you executed during previous sessions. You have not learned how to see these commands or use them. If you are interested in learning this trick now, you can examine the chapter on the Korn shell or the C shell program.

CHAPTER 3

1. You might have just answered the prompt: *enter user name* or some such prompt. You might have come through the network via the **telnet** or **rlogin** commands—which you haven't learned, but could look up in chapter 12.

2. You would use the command **pwd** to determine the name of the current directory that would be your home directory if you had just logged in. This directory is special because it is the directory that will store your files. This directory is chosen for you by the UNIX system administrator.

3. You would use the **ls** command to start with. But this command does not show you if there are any files that start with a ".". To show all files in a directory, you would need to use the command **ls -a**. The files that start with a "." are used to create your specific user environment.

4. You would use a slightly different command to determine what the various "things" found in your directory are. The command **ls -aF** will indicate whether these are files or directories.

5. You would use the command **cd /bin**.

6. You would use the command **ls -aCF** to list the contents of your directory in columns. You should find that there are several files in your home directory that start with a ".".

7. You would use the command **cd /usr/marty** or you would use the command **cd ~** where the "~" has a special meaning of the home directory of the user that is logged in.

8. You might recognize the name of the diskette drive as */dev/rfd0*. This directory also contains the names of all the serial devices such as */dev/tty1*, */dev/tty5*.

9. You would use the command **cd ~**.

10. File systems that have names that contain ":" are not actually on your local system. The amount of available disk space is the amount available in the file system in which you are working. Free space in other file systems is not available to you.

CHAPTER 4

1. Use the command **cat < inv** to create a file with input from the keyboard. Use the CTRL+D keys to end the **cat** command and save the file.

2. Use the command **mkdir INV**, **mkdir ORD**, and so on. You would not be able to create the file *inv* and the directory *INV* because on DOS systems filenames are not case sensitive.

3. Use the **ls** command to show whether *inv* is a file or a directory. You know the file is there if the **ls** command displays its attributes. You would use some form of the **ls** command, either **ls -aCF** or **ls -l** to see which are files and which are directories.

4. You will not be able to create a file with the same name as a directory (or vice versa).

5. Again use the **ls** command to display attributes of a file or directory. If the object of interest no longer exists, the **ls** command will display an error.

6. You verify what directory you are in with the **pwd** command. You can create a subdirectory with the same name as another directory. You just cannot create an object in the same subdirectory with the name of an object that already exists.

7. The **-Caf** options are particularly useful in examining files in a directory.

8. You might not know how to examine the contents for a text file since this topic is actually not covered until the next chap-

ter. Use the **more** or **cat** command to display the contents of a text file. You probably do not know how to compare the contents of two files in UNIX. That subject is also covered in chapter 5. As a hint, you would use the **diff** command.

9. You would use the command **mv inv INV1**. Use a form of the **ls** command to show that the file is in two directories. You might try the command **ls /usr/marty/inv /usr/martya/INV1**.

10. You copied one from the other; they had better be the same. These two commands will have the same effect as the **mv** command.

11. You would use a command like **ls i***. You would use the command **ls ??**.

12. You would use the command **chmod u+rwx ***. No one besides the owner will be able to read or write these files.

13. The attributes of a directory are set by the current value of the **umask**. You would use the command **cp file testdir** to copy a file into a directory. If you did not spell the name of a directory, then the **cp** command would create another file with that name containing whatever was in the original file.

14. You will be able to create a file and make "root" its owner. But you will not be able to change the file's owner back to you.

CHAPTER 5

1. You would use the **cat** command or if you have peeked and looked at chapter 6 you could use the **vi** command.

2. You would display the entire file with the **cat** command. You would display the first line with the command: **head 1 file** and the last line of the file with the command: **tail 1 file**.

3. You would merge the two files into a third with the command **cat file1 file2 > file3**.

4. You would search the file with the command: **grep lion file**. You must specify exactly how the string is found in the file. You would display the line the match is found on with the command **grep -n lion file**.

5. You would print the list with the command: **lp file**. You would print only the first two entries with the command: **head 2 file | lp**. You would print only those entries that contain the string "ige" with the command: **grep ige file | lp**.

6. You would determine your default printer with the **lpstat** command. You print a text file with the **lp** command. You would cancel a print job with the **cancel** command.

CHAPTER 6

1. When you start **vi**, the initial message indicates whether this is a new file or not.

2. Don't forget to get into input mode with a "i" character. Even though you are editing a new file that is empty, **vi** does not automatically put you into the input mode.

3. Put your cursor under the first character in "men". The command is **cw** and you are then in input mode and can enter the characters "people" and push the escape key to get out of input mode. Reverse two characters with the **xp** command. Put cursor under the first character in the phrase "to come to" and then enter the **i** command and type in the phrase you want to add. Exit input mode with the escape key as usual.

4. Carriage returns are the same as any input. Put your cursor just after the word "available." Get into input mode and enter a carriage return and then touch the escape key to end input mode. You join two lines with the **J** command.

5. Copy the two lines that you have by moving your cursor onto the first line of interest and entering the **yy2** command. To add the two lines enter the **p** command. To save the file as "aid" you would use the **:w aid** command. To exit from **vi** you would enter the **:q** command.

6. You would edit the *first* file with the command **vi first**. You can enter each line as shown or you can create the first line and copy that line five times and then go back and change the one word in each line that needs changing.

7. You would read in the *aid* file after the third line by positioning your cursor at the beginning of the fourth line and issuing the **:r aid** command. You would indent each of the lines from the *aid* file with the **:.,.+3s/^/ /** command.

8. The file you have created should look like:

```
This is the first line.
This is the second line.
```

```
        Now is the time for all good people who are all
        available to come to the aid of their country.
This is the third line.
This is the fourth line.
        Now is the time for all good people who are all
        available to come to the aid of their country.
This is the fifth line.
This is the sixth line.
```

Moving text is done by deleting it from its current place and inserting it at the new place.

CHAPTER 7

1. One command to create such a list would be **ls -lR > myfiles**. Another command would be **find . -print > myfiles**.
2. This sequence of commands creates a file called *assorted*, which will contain seven lines. You can determine that with the **wc** command.
3. Use the command **mail john < letter**.
4. You would only see those processes that you started in this session.
5. The *-f* and *-l* options provide the most information, with each providing a different set of data. You would need the *-e* option to get information on *every* process.
6. One way to do this is to use the command **ps -umarty** if your user id is "marty." You could also issue the **ps -e | grep marty** commands to see what processes belong to the user *marty*.
7. The command would look like **sort -u animals | tee animals.sort | more**.
8. The first cron file would look like

```
00 04 * * 1,2,3,4,5,6 got_to_make_the_donuts
```

The second cron file would be

```
00   00,02,04,06,08,10 * * 1,2,3,4,5
got_to_make_the_coffee
00   12,14,16,18,20,22 * * 1,2,3,4,5
got_to_make_the_coffee
```

```
00   00,01,02,03,04,05 * * 6 got_to_make_the_coffee
00   06,07,08,09,10,11 * * 6 got_to_make_the_coffee
00   12,13,14,15,16,17 * * 6 got_to_make_the_coffee
00   18,19,20,21,22,23 * * 6 got_to_make_thc_coffee
00   00,04,08,12,16,20 * * 0 got_to_make_the_coffee
```

The spacing is arbitary.

CHAPTER 8

1. You would use the command **echo $SHELL** to display which shell program is managing your terminal session. To change to a different shell program, you would just execute it. You would use the command **echo $PROMPT** to determine command line prompt. You can expect that certain command line prompts are usually for a particular shell program but you should not depend on that.

2. A large number of shell programs exist. This book only discusses the three most common shell programs but many others have been written. As in the case of other competing programs, every UNIX person has his or her idea of what a shell program does and a number have actually carried out their ideas. You can find these other shell programs on the Internet at archives that keep UNIX programs.

3. Did you include files that are in subdirectories of your home directory? If you know how to use the program **grep**, you could search for the name of the file of interest in a text file that contained the name of all the files in your home directory.

4. Shell programs exist for DOS systems. The batch scripting language is much richer on UNIX systems than on DOS systems.

CHAPTER 9

1. You would create the directory with: **mkdir bscript**. The shell script would look like

#!/bin/ksh
if [-a $1]
then

```
        if [ -d $1 ]
        then
            cd $1
        else
            echo $1 is not a directory
            exit 2
        fi
    else
        echo $1 does not exist
        exit 1
    fi
    echo This new directory is `pwd`
    cd -
```

You could perform other tests to insure that the directory is accessible.

2. You create a subdirectory with **mkdir bin**. Move the new script to the *bin* directory with **mv bscript/new bin/new**. Make it executable with **chmod a+x bin/new**. Execute with the command **bin/new bscript** to test if you can access the *bscript* directory.

3. Set up history with **HISTSIZE=10**.

CHAPTER 10

1. You would set up the history size to be 10 with the command **set history=10**. You display commands in history with the **history** command. You can execute a previous command with the **!ls** command.

2. You would make that directory with **kmkdir cscript** command. You would move to that directory with the **cd script** command. You would create the *bin* directory in your home directory with the command **mkdir $HOME/bin**. You would add this to your *PATH* variable with **set path= ($path $HOME/bin)** command.

3. The script would look like

```
#!/bin/csh
if ( -d $1 )
then
    pushd $1
    echo This is `pwd` directory
```

```
    ls -l
    popd
else
    ccho $1 is not a directory
endif
```

The command would be **mv new bin**. You would use the command **chmod a+x bin/new**. You would execute it with the command **bin/new**.

CHAPTER 11

1. You should be able to use the command: **mail marick** where *marick* should be replaced with your user name. The system will send mail to any user that you choose. One way to save a message to process later is to forward that message to yourself.
2. Once you have mail to read, you can use the **mail** command without any other options to read your mail.
3. Use the **d** subcommand.
4. The message ends up in the user's mailbox. That user will not know to read his or her mail until he or she signs into the system on which he or she reads mail.
5. Your friend would use the same command as in answer 1.
6. If the user is logged into the system, the shell program will notify that user of the delivery of mail.
7. You can create a message to any user that you wish. The **mail** program does not verify the existence of any user. The mail delivery system will attempt to deliver that message. If the delivery fails, you will be notified and the message will be returned to you. The delivery of a message to a set of users will proceed in parallel and the failure of delivery to one user will not cause any other message not to be delivered.
8. Using a subject will help to remind you to read that message.
9. You would create a letter in a file using the **vi** command. You would mail that to yourself with: **mail myself < myletter**.
10. The **mail** command formats the message for you and adds some header information.
11. You need to help the mail delivery system know to which system to send your message in order to deliver it to the user

you intended. Thus, the full address of a user contains not only the user's name but a system on which that user is known.

CHAPTER 12

1. You would display the file systems on your local UNIX host with the **df** command. You can tell that file systems are not local by looking at the "Filesystem" column in the output from the **df** command. If the name of the file system contains a colon, that file system is not local. Yes, you can make file systems on a remote UNIX system available locally if the remote UNIX system supports network file systems.

2. You can use either **telnet** or **rlogin** to connect to a remote UNIX host from another UNIX host. **telnet** provides a number of options that may be useful. You can copy a file from one system to another by using either the **rcp** command or the **ftp** command.

3. You might be able to use network file system services. You would use the **df** command to examine what file systems are mounted on a system which you can sign onto. If the appropriate file system is mounted, you could use a simple **cp** command to copy files.

CHAPTER 13

1. You would use the **uname** command to be sure that you are on the system you expect to be on. UNIX systems are aware of what method was used to connect to the system but treat all connections the same.

CHAPTER 14

1. You can use the **file** command to determine if a particular binary file is executable on the cpu on which you are testing. On other processors the **file** command will only return that the file is binary data but will not indicate on which processor this file is executable. Just because a file has the execut-

able attribute turned on does not mean it is actually an executable.

2. The command to place all of your files and directories in your home directory on a diskette would be **tar cvf /dev/ rfd0 ***. You can check on what is on the diskette with the command: **tar tvf /dev/rfd0**.

3. The command would be **tar cvf /dev/rfd0 memo1 docs/ manual1 docs/ord.12 source/helloworld.c**. Another choice would be **tar cvf /dev/rfd0 memo1 -C docs manual1 ord.12 -C source helloworld.c**. The contents of the second diskette will have no relative directory names for the *manual1*, *ord.12*, and *helloworld.c* files.

4. The command would be **doscp * a:** or **doswrite * /dev/ rfd0**. Obviously, you would use **dir a:** or **dir b:**.

5. The command would be **ln /usr/marty/temp /usr/marty/tmp**. The command you would use is **ls /usr/marty/temp /usr/ marty/tmp**. You can tell they are linked because the count of links (the second column from the left) is not "1" but "2."

6. The disk space shown in the **df** command can contain disk space that is not physically on the system you are currently executing on.

7. Diskettes on UNIX systems are not formatted the same. On UNIX systems you can have diskettes that can be read by DOS systems. On DOS systems all diskettes are formatted the same. In general, you should be able to read a tar-formatted diskette on any UNIX system.

CHAPTER 15

1. You would use the **ftp** command to retrieve a file from an archive server. You would use the **cd** command to change to the directory of interest and the **get** command to retrieve a file.

2. Script might look something like

```
#!/bin/csh -f
#
#  3 Parameters on command line
#     1.  Name of host
#     2.  Directory file is in
```

```
#       3.  Name of file to retrieve
#
echo "" >> /tmp/$$M
#  Send user name and password
echo "user anonymous marick@mycompany.com"
                                        >> /tmp/$$M
#  Get into directory of interest
echo "cd $2" >> /tmp/$$M
#  Get a list of contents of directory
echo "ls -C" >> /tmp/$$M
#  Get file of interest
echo "get $3" >> /tmp/$$M
#  End your ftp session
echo "quit" >> /tmp/$$M
#  Now go do the ftp operation
ftp -nv $1 < /tmp/$$M >& $1.out
#  Save return code from ftp operation
setenv ST $status
sleep 10
if ( $ST == 0 ) rm /tmp/$$M
#
```

Quick Comparison of DOS and UNIX Commands

OVERVIEW

Sometimes remembering which UNIX command does what can be frustrating. The tables on the next several pages offer several different ways to determine what command you want to use to perform the desired operation. Table B.1 is organized by which function you wish to perform. Table B.2 is organized by which DOS command you want to perform on the UNIX system. Table B.3 is organized by which UNIX command you want to perform on the DOS system. In all of the following tables, commands should be entered on the same command line even if the command is shown on two lines in the table.

Table B.1.   Which UNIX Command to Use for a Particular DOS Command

DOS Command	UNIX Command	Operation
attrib [options] file1	chmod [options] file1	Change attributes of file
cd	pwd	Present working directory
cd dir1	cd dir1	Change working directory
comp file1 file2	diff file1 file2	Compare two text files
copy con: file1	cat > file1	Create a text file from keyboard
copy file1 file2	cp file1 file2	Copy a file
copy file1+file2 file3	cat file1 file2 > file3	Combine two text files into one
date	date	Display date
del file1	rm file1	Delete a file
deltree dir1	rm -rf dir1	Delete a directory and its files
dir	ls	Display contents of directory
dir file1	ls -l file1	Display attributes of file
echo Message	echo Message	Display message on terminal
edit file1	vi file1	Edit a text file
find string file	grep string file	Search text file for "string"
md dir1	mkdir dir1	Create a directory
more < file1	more file1	Display a text file
move dir1 newdir	mv dir1 newdir	Rename a directory
print file1	lp file1	Print a file
rename file1 file2	mv file1 file2	Rename a file
rd dir1	rmdir dir1	Delete a directory
sort < file1 > newfile	sort -i file1 -o newfile	Sorting a text file
time	date	Display time of day
type file1	cat file1	Write a file to screen

Table B.2.   Which DOS Command to Use for a Particular UNIX Command

UNIX Command	DOS Command	Operation
cat > file1	copy con file1	Create a text file from keyboard
cat file1	type file1	Write a file to screen
cat file1 file2 > file3	copy file1+file2 file3	Combine two text files into one
cd dir1	cd dir1	Change working directory
chmod [options] file1	attrib [options] file1	Change attributes of file
cp file1 file2	copy file1 file2	Copy a file
date	date	Display date
diff file1 file2	comp file1 file2	Compare two text files
echo Message	echo Message	Display message on terminal
grep string file	find string file	Search text file for "string"
lp file1	print file1	Print a file
ls	dir	Display contents of directory
ls -l file1	dir file1	Display attributes of file
mkdir dir1	md dir1	Create a directory
more file1	more < file1	Display a text file
mv file1 file2	rename file1 file2	Rename a file
mv dir1 newdir	(N/A)	Rename a directory
pwd	cd	Present working directory
rmdir dir1	rd dir1	Delete a directory
rm -rf dir1	deltree dir1	Delete a directory and its files
rm file1	del file1	Delete a file
sort -i file1 -o newfile	sort < file1 > newfile	Sorting a text file
vi file1	edit file1	Edit a text file

Table B.3. Which UNIX and DOS Command to Use for a Particular Operation

Desired Operation	DOS Command	UNIX Command
Change attributes of file	attrib [options] file1	chmod [options] file1
Change working directory	cd dir1	cd dir1
Combine two text files into one	copy file1+file2 file3	cat file1 file2 > file3
Compare two text files	comp file1 file2	diff file1 file2
Copy a file	copy file1 file2	cp file1 file2
Create a directory	md dir1	mkdir dir1
Create a text file from keyboard	copy con: file1	cat > file1
Delete a directory	rd dir1	rmdir dir1
Delete a directory and its files	deltree dir1	rm -rf dir1
Delete a file	del file1	rm file1
Display attributes of file	dir file1	ls -l file1
Display contents of directory	dir	ls
Display date	date	date
Display Message on Terminal	echo Message	echo Message
Display text file	more < file1	more file1
Display time of day	time	date
Display working directory	cd	pwd
Edit a text file	edit file1	vi file1
Print a file	print file1	lp file1
Rename a directory	move dir1 newdir	mv dir1 newdir
Rename a file	rename file1 file2 move C:file1 file2	mv file1 file2
Search text file for "string"	find string file	grep string file
Sort a text file	sort < file1 > newfile	sort -i file1 -o newfile
Write a file to screen	type file1	cat file1

Index